BREAKING UP WITH THE BAD GIRL
And All That Chains You

IMANI WADE

Breaking up with the Bad Girl And All That Chains You
Copyright © 2019 by Imani Wade. All rights reserved.

Editing by S'ambrosia Wasike
Book design and cover design by Next Page

First published in the United States on December 1, 2019
ISBN: 978-0-578-61196-9

Unless otherwise noted, all scriptures are taken from the NEW INTERNATIONAL VERSION (NIV): Scripture taken from THE HOLY BIBLE, NEW INTERNATIONAL VERSION ®. Copyright© 1973, 1978, 1984, 2011 by Biblica, Inc.™. Used by permission of Zondervan

Scriptures marked NLT are taken from the HOLY BIBLE, NEW LIVING TRANSLATION (NLT): Scriptures taken from the HOLY BIBLE, NEW LIVING TRANSLATION, Copyright© 1996, 2004, 2007 by Tyndale House Foundation. Used by permission of Tyndale House Publishers, Inc., Carol Stream, Illinois 60188. All rights reserved. Used by permission.

Scriptures marked ESV are taken from the THE HOLY BIBLE, ENGLISH STANDARD VERSION (ESV): Scriptures taken from THE HOLY BIBLE, ENGLISH STANDARD VERSION ® Copyright© 2001 by Crossway, a publishing ministry of Good News Publishers. Used by permission.

Scriptures marked NKJV are taken from the NEW KING JAMES VERSION (NKJV): Scripture taken from the NEW KING JAMES VERSION®. Copyright© 1982 by Thomas Nelson, Inc. Used by permission. All rights reserved.

Scripture quotations marked TPT are from The Passion Translation®. Copyright © 2017, 2018 by Passion & Fire Ministries, Inc. Used by permission. All rights reserved. ThePassionTranslation.com.

All rights reserved. No part of the material protected by this copyright may be reproduced or utilized in any form by any means, electronic or mechanical, including photocopying, recording, or by any information storage and retrieval system without permission in writing from the copyright owner. Contact Imani Wade for permission to make copies of any part of this work.

Dedicated to my dad- Our relationship is an answered prayer that my youngest self always longed for. The restoration we have proves that God still answers prayers and that our faith is not in vain. Thank you for being honest and for encouraging me to share my story for His glory.

I love you.

This book is a memoir that's based on real events. It reflects my present recollections of experiences over time, and it includes some mature content. Some names and characteristics have been changed, some events have been compressed, and some dialogue has been recreated.

Contents

	Prologue	i
1.	Life as a Stripper	1
2.	Life as a Pre-Teen/Teenager	13
3.	Becoming His	25
4.	Blasts From Your Past	37
5.	Breaking up with the Bad Girl	47
6.	The Bad Girl Blues	65
7.	Mindset Makeover	77
8.	The "Good Girl" Identity Crisis	91

9. Giving Them Grace, When You Want to Slap Them in the Face! 103

10. Trusting THEM 115

11. The Dangers of Detachment 129

12. Playing Tug-of-War with God 139

13. Way Maker, Miracle Worker, Promise Keeper .. 153

14. Remaining His 163

15. Epilogue 171

16. Acknowledgements 173

17. Resources for Sharing Your Story 177

18. Quick Prayers for Writing/Sharing Your Story . 181

19. Scriptures for the Soul 183

20. About Imani 187

Prologue

As I lifted my head to gaze at the stars floating so far above me in the universe, the wind gently brushed my cheek. The stars glistened brightly against the dark night sky; so far away, yet so near to me. It was in that moment, when I was captivated by their beauty and in complete admiration of God's artistic abilities, that I heard the Holy Spirit whisper to me:

> *You are just as unique as they are, Imani. From your laugh to the way that you love people, you are just as unique. Your heart is unique, your personality is unique, and your story is unique. You are just as unique as they are, my daughter.*

I smiled, but then the battle with Satan's lies began. *How could I be that unique?* Words like **lonely**, **critical**, and **bruised** attempted to replace the words the Holy Spirit had just spoken to my heart. The wrestling match continued in my mind until I finally chose to silence the lies and listen to the truth that I had just heard. Isn't it wild how quick the enemy is to shoot his arrows at us? Sometimes it's enough to make me want to scream, "Can I get a break, please?" While the idea of a break from Satan's lies is cute, it is not realistic. I had to choose to believe the truth. I had to not only hear God, but actually listen to Him.

I am not lonely, critical, or bruised. Yes, there are times I feel so alone that I just want to cry and curl up in a ball, and then sleep until the following day. But I am not lonely. Yes, I struggle with perfectionism and control and can be very critical of myself and others. But I am not critical. And yes, after being healed from one hurt, I find the situation has left a bruise on my heart that pops up to the surface again, and again, and again. But I am not bruised.

These are all real struggles that I have, but they do not represent who I am or how God views me. You heard our Father. I am just as unique as the stars in the sky. You and I both are. This includes our journey, our stories, our personalities, and our hearts. My greatest desire, as you read my book, is that you feel understood as you connect on a deeper level with God.

In closing, I want to say thank you. Thank you for picking up this book and for being supportive of my journey. Thank you for allowing me to be real with you. This was not an easy journey, yet it has blessed me in tremendous ways. I hope it does for you as well. In the back of the book, you will find Bible verses to encourage you and resources to help you share your own story. There are also resources to bring you one step closer to God as you develop into the woman He has created you to be.

Chapter 1
LIFE AS A STRIPPER

Grabbing the sides of the plush velvet seat, I adjusted my body on top of the drunk man. If I planned on getting any money from this man, I needed to be desirable. I needed to make sure that I was sitting at the perfect angle and that I looked slender yet curvy at all times. He continued sipping his beer, the stench of alcohol and cigarettes staining his breath. Emboldened by the alcohol, he began to compliment me and share pointless information about himself. His eyes constantly shifted from my face to my breasts.

Count… to… ten.

He was stretching my patience. There was a potential amount of money I could make each night, and I had developed a routine to ensure that every time I worked, I would achieve that goal. Typically, I would sit with a man for two—sometimes three—songs, listening intently for the DJ's announcement of the next song while pretending to care about whatever the man was sharing with me. If the man was feeling me by the end of the song limit, then I would invite him backstage for a dance. That is where I made most of my money. This guy had one more song before I would take him to get a dance. But he was one of those guys—the type who wanted attention, conversation, admiration, and affection if I expected to get any of his money. Were the twenty dollars even worth it?

I wasn't tipsy enough, and he wasn't cute or intriguing enough for me to even pretend that I cared about how long his week had been. I scanned the room for tequila. Everyone was drinking beer. It was early on a Friday night, and people were just starting to trickle into the club—both men and women. As women walked into the club, they would usually give me a glare of distaste. I would always respond with a sardonic yet seductive look, as I took note of which ladies would be easy to break and which ones were probably going to remain bitter the entire night.

The second song was coming to an end, but this guy was not trying to go anywhere. He was messing up my game plan. He cocked his head back, laughing at something his friend said. The stripper on his friend's lap was more engaging than I was. Somehow she was managing to keep the entire group of men entertained—including the man I was sitting on. What was his name again? His dry hand touched my lower back. I cringed, wondering what his hand had been doing throughout the night. His hand lowered, the dryness of his palm resembling the dryness creeping up my throat as I sat there, sober. I hated being touched, but I resolved to shut my eyes and focus on my goal for the night.

Count... to... ten. Breathe.

It was working. I could feel the animosity leaving my body as I exhaled. This method of relaxation was something I had started using at the beginning of the year as part of a decision I had made to be intentional about overcoming my anger issues. After going to jail and catching a felony due to violence, I knew I needed to change. Releasing my anger through fighting was not smart, and I needed a healthier form of release. Aside from taking deep breaths, I had also begun reading "The Purpose Driven Life", and from time to time, I would think about a particular Bible verse it mentioned:

My dear brothers and sisters, take note of this: Everyone should be quick to listen, slow to speak and slow to become angry, because human anger does not produce the righteousness that God desires.

- James 1:19-20

As much as I wanted to change, I doubted that I could ever actually apply this verse to my life. Maybe it would be easier for someone who didn't have so much to be angry about, but I had been fighting my fate all of my life. It didn't help, either, that I was always surrounded at the club by incompetent, horny men who often insulted and easily angered me. I knew that I would remain a belligerent person as long as I stayed in this lifestyle, but I just needed to survive five more years so I could make enough money to quit and move on to opening my dream salon.

Count... to... ten.

I placed my hand on the back of the man's head and whispered gently into his ear, prompting him to go backstage with me.

"But you just got here," he whined. "Have a beer and just sit with me for a minute." His words stung and struck me with disrespect, like the cigarette stench from his mouth. He moved his hand from my lower back to my thigh to give me a reassuring pat, and my entire nerve struck.

Count... to... te-

"Listen, you're not spending any money, and you're drinking cheap beer. Nobody wants that nasty ass drink! Do you really think I want to sit here for thirty minutes listening to how pitiful your life is? Nah, I am too fine for that, and you owe me for my precious time. Go put some lotion on those dry hands. If you think touching on us with those crusty hands is turning us on, you are sadly mistaken." I hopped off of him and snatched the twenty-dollar-bill from his table. "You owe me this for my time. I'm too fine for this stupid mess," I said, as I flipped my twenty-six-inch weave and grabbed my mini pink Guess purse. In near shock, the man tried to get my attention by yelling my name as I rushed to the locker room, hoping that there would be weed or a drink waiting for me.

"Layna, what happened?" Montana asked, as she licked her fingers to separate the one dollar bills from the tens. "You look like you're about to beat someone's ass."

She and I were the most attractive black women at the club, and although we would tag team at times, she was still considered my competition. She was beautiful, shorter than me, and curvy. Being tall in platform stripper heels often turned men away, so if they desired a petite, light-skinned black woman, they would reject me and run to Montana. Although this would often cause my insecurities to scream, I would always help her whenever possible, and she would do the same for me. That particular night, I needed $400 to pay for my car note, and Montana had her own personal matters she needed to handle.

"Do you need some weed, girl?" she asked, as she propped one leg up on the bench and leaned over to re-apply her Versace perfume. She sprayed her entire body to ensure that her scent was enticing. "Like, what's up? You're heated right now, and you know you won't make any money tonight with an attitude like that. I can get you some weed or a bar. Just let me know what you need."

"Girl, the last time I popped a bar, I went to jail. Not doing that again," I laughed as I spritzed Marc Jacobs Daisy behind my neck and onto my lower back. "But I could use some weed and some money."

"Damn, girl. You know how these men are. Just spend more time letting them talk about themselves, caress their head every now and then, and give it four songs. It's a slow start, but at least you'll make some money. Let's smoke, and then we can go find a table with tequila. Take some shots before you go on stage, and let's make this money."

"I'm down. I have five more girls ahead of me before I have to get on stage," I replied, twirling around to check myself out before we walked out to the patio. Everything about me needed to be flawless. I was going to have to get on stage soon, and sharing the stage with other women always fed my insecurities. There were six stages with six women per stage. Men would typically go from stage to stage, eager to give money to the woman that they desired. I hated going up there sober—Layna danced better when her ego was fed with alcohol—but it also didn't help that I would have to compete with other women as we all tried to work for our worth.

"When you're done with all six stages, come find me," Montana said, as she handed me some weed. "I have a table, and I may try to get the guys to come tip you. It's a bachelor party full of white cowboys that requested two black girls and one blondie."

I inhaled the weed, hoping that these men weren't going to reject me and waste my time as well. My anxiety was now laced with anger. So much for counting to ten. I was just praying that it would all end one day.

I WOKE UP FEELING LIKE an 18-wheeler had run over my body and then reversed and parked on top of me. My legs were typically sore after dancing six to eight-hour shifts, but now my back and neck were aching too. *Why was I feeling so sore and tired?* The cowboys knew how to party—taking back moonshine and beers as we danced with them the entire night. Their bachelor party had reminded me of why I hated men. I watched in disgust as another stripper led the soon-to-be-married man to the back for his "final day of being a free man". I knew exactly what would happen next. After all, I was familiar with selling my own body—

"You know, if you move to Cali without me, you will have a lot of competition. Too many light-skinned shorties move out there, trying to get some bands like you," said Antwan, as he leaned back on my bed watching me get dressed. "But with me by your side, I can get you some ball players and bread. Get ya name out there, too. Just think about it."

I flirted with the idea for a moment, but decided against going with him. I recognized his game and his charm. He was trying to pimp me. He definitely wasn't the first or the last man who had offered me a "dream", but he was the most insulting of the six. He left that day telling me that I was dumb without him and that I wouldn't go far because I wasn't that pretty anyway. His words pierced my heart, watering the seed of rejection that had already been rooted there for some time. I instantly fixed my facial expression, hoping that he couldn't tell that his words had done so much damage. After buckling his pants, he threw a wad of money on my nightstand and murmured a few more insults as he left my apartment. I immediately swallowed the shame and regret, choosing instead to cloud my thoughts with more weed.

BACK AT THE BACHELOR PARTY, the other stripper emerged from the VIP room an hour later with a blank expression on her face. I knew that look very well. A mixture of anger and sadness—not too far off from what she was probably feeling in that moment—crept into my heart. I reached for my bag and spritzed more perfume onto my neck to distract myself. Even though I felt a certain amount of sympathy for her, I also found myself loathing her for the amount of money she made, her fake breasts, and her petite frame. She didn't need to do extra for money. She was one of the prettiest girls in the club. I wondered if it was her choice or if she had a pimp forcing her to prostitute herself. I knew some strippers had pimps. One of my closest stripper friends did. I looked over at Montana as she danced, completely out of her mind.

My mind was spiraling out of control, as memories of Montana's bruised body—the result of her pimp's abuse—resurfaced. I fought back this memory only to have it replaced by another painful memory of a customer thrusting himself on a woman who was lying motionless in the VIP booth beside me. Once I had realized what was happening, I stopped dancing and charged at him. He was raping a drugged up woman! Chills rain up my arms, and I felt myself fading in and out. Unaware of how to handle my own emotions at that moment, I took three more shots of moonshine. Soon, I blacked out.

My back pain intensified as I rose from the bed in my cluttered apartment. "Ughhh, whyyy?" I groaned. My heels had been thrown near the front door, and my clothes were spread all over my bedroom floor. *How did I get home last night?* Probably the same way I did every night I left the club; with a little bit of hope and a lot of mint gum to cover the alcohol on my breath. Driving home drunk at 4 a.m. had become a skill for me, and I was starting to believe that I had an angel protecting me.

    Rolling over to the side of my bed, I reached for my nightstand to find my weed. I had just enough left to get me through the day, but I needed to buy more at work later. I inhaled the smoke from my pipe and held it in before slowly exhaling. Dragging my feet to find my purse, I rifled through the money I had made the night before and found the Adderall. *Magic, yes!* I had bought enough pills from a dealer I had met at the club to get me through the next week. He had offered a good deal on weed and pills if I offered free dances, so I agreed. I popped the pill back and dry swallowed it, ready to feel like Superwoman. I usually dealt with hangovers by exercising with my personal trainer, smoking weed, or doing light yoga, but this time I needed something to fix the pain I was feeling.

    My head was throbbing, as a stiff pain continued to creep up my neck. To make matters worse, my body temperature also began to rise, bringing about one of my worst fears: getting sick on a Saturday when I had money to make. I had only made

$400 the night before, which was enough to cover my car note, but I still needed to make rent money, and I had to get my nails done. They were starting to look trashy. I did not have time to get sick, but the more I tried to fight it, the stronger the pain felt. So, I laid back down on my bed and surrendered to the sickness. Battling with restlessness, I picked up my book.

And we know that in all things God works for the good of those who love Him, who have been called according to His purpose.

- Romans 8:28

I stared at these words for about two minutes, trying to dissect their meaning. I really wanted to know God, but I also needed to understand why He had created me. *Those who are called according to His purpose? How do you know if you're called?* I wondered. *And if I am really loved by this God, why does my life feel like a joke?* Angrily, I tossed the book to the side, feeling too messy for this "loving" God.

TWO WEEKS LATER, I sat in my car as the rain roared from the sky, violently pounding on my window. *Ugh.* I was too high for this. It had been a week since a SWAT team had flooded my former club and shut it down for forty-five days. According to the news and the girls in the locker room, a customer had overdosed on drugs from a drug deal made in our club. After undercover cops had come through to investigate, they sent in a SWAT team with German Shepherds to raid the club.

"What the hell? Why are the lights on?" a girl yelled as she sat with her client.

As soon as I realized what was happening, I ran to the locker room to grab my clothes, weed, and keys. Other strippers with warrants or drugs ran to the back to disappear before they were caught by the police. It was a mad-house.

The rain intensified, my heart matching its pace as I pulled into the parking lot. I had already tried looking for work at four other clubs in the city, but I had been rejected by all of them.

"We have too many black girls right now. I'm sorry."

"You need to drop a few pounds, but you can waitress, if you want."

"Yeah, you just have too many tattoos."

"If you work here, you'll have to work for me too."

This was my last option. If I wasn't going to get hired here, I was going to have to try for the dayshift at a few other clubs in the morning. I tucked my weave into my hood, grabbed my backpack, and sprinted for the door. Music blared from the lobby, as I entered. The door girl looked me up and down before grabbing her walkie-talkie to summon the manager. Moments later, two men arrived and escorted me to their office.

"You're pretty," the tall man said. His short, stocky colleague remained seated behind his desk not saying a word. Before I could say anything, the tall one got straight to the point.

"You plan to work tonight, right?"

"Yes, tonight and through the weekend." I followed closely behind him as he gave me a brief tour of the stages and the VIP sections. We ended the tour in the locker room. The shorter man still hadn't said a word.

"Your mandatory work days are Sunday or Monday, if you plan to work the weekend. We want you here at least four days out of the week, do you understand?" *Finally he speaks.*

I gave him an obligatory nod, knowing that I was not going to be able to commit to his schedule. The night classes I was enrolled in were a higher priority for me. I wanted to get my real estate license, and once I did, I could use the money I made from flipping houses to fund my dream salon. He and his club could live without me.

"Sounds like a plan. Thanks again." I smiled and walked past them, ready to find a drink to get my mind right for the night.

WEEKS HAD PASSED since I had begun working at the new club, and the amount of money I was making there wasn't even close to what I had been making at my former club. Girls were stealing clients, managers were demanding larger tips, and the work schedule was overwhelming. I hated it there. I hated the people. I hated myself.

After another long Saturday night, I threw my bag in the backseat of my car and slid into the driver's seat, ready to go home. I had agreed to go to a church the next morning.

Great idea, Imani, I berated myself. *Just brilliant.* I knew I was going to be hungover. *Hungover in a church. Might as well burn me while I'm there.* I grabbed my phone to text Amanda to tell her I couldn't make it, but before I could press send, I exited out of the app and tossed my phone to the side. I had already canceled on her before, and if I did it again, I would feel terrible.

"Damn it!" I shouted. I had no choice. "Lord, please let me wake up feeling good tomorrow." I gripped the steering wheel, trying to conjure up a quick hangover cure. Adderall was no longer an option, since I had decided to only turn to it in emergencies. At least when I looked in the mirror, my makeup still looked fresh. Of course it was fresh. I had barely made any money that night. I rolled my eyes at the thought of the morons in the club that had denied any dances because they just wanted to drink and talk.

"So go to a bar," I had said to one guy, after taking his shot of tequila. I slammed the shot glass down and walked off irritated at the thought that it was going to be one of those nights... again.

Frustrated, I began to cry in my car. Why hadn't I just gone to a four-year university after high school like every other "good girl"? Why did I have to get arrested and catch a felony? I mean, what eighteen-year-old female from a good home does that? Why did I have to be myself right now? Tears fell down my cheeks, the hot moisture hitting my hand as I wiped my face.

"This sucks. I suck. My life sucks. Ugh! I am so stupid. Why did I even have to be born? I hate my life. Just take me out, God. I'm done!" By this time I was shouting and shaking. But there was no one around to hear my broken heart; no one to hear my hurt; no one to hear the little girl inside of me, crying for her loss of innocence and desperately seeking another chance at life.

Chapter 2
LIFE AS A PRE-TEEN/TEENAGER

"Imani, did he or did he not rape you?" my dad pressed, with my stepmother, Cynthia, standing beside him.

Their bedroom felt like it was closing in on me. At that moment, I would have actually preferred to be crushed by the bedroom's brick walls than to be standing there in front of them. I could have even traded places with Maxwell, our Rottweiler. He laid there beside my father's feet, breathing heavily with a big grin on his face. *Must be nice, Max. Life is so easy for you.* It hadn't been easy for me.

As a twelve-year-old girl, I had already experienced so much more pain than what God had intended for me. I was being raised by a single mom, while screaming for my dad to be present in my life—the same dad who had randomly popped up at Braum's, of all places, with an entirely new family. On top of that, the ins and outs of my hormones had never been properly explained to me, so as a result, I struggled with understanding my cycle and the sexual urges I had begun to feel after being raped. Full of malice, I was ready to shut down and hide or erupt with anger at any time.

My eyes searched the room, afraid to look at my dad or Cynthia. *Why was this happening?* My palms were sweating, and strands of my hair stuck to the back of my neck.

"Imani Wade!" he shouted, his voice filled with anger and hurt. He looked like he was ready to kill him. *Him.*

I had met him in the teen service at church. Even though I was only twelve, I didn't like going to the service for my age group, so I decided to be with the older guys. I was turning thirteen in a few months anyway, and it wasn't like they were going to ask for proof of my age. Apparently, I also looked fifteen, so that worked for me as well. That was the age that I gave him, anyway.

He thought I was pretty, and he complimented my hair. He noticed me, and that was all that I needed. Late at night, I would wait for my mom to fall asleep before sneaking on the phone to talk to him. I had been caught once, and I knew my mom would spank me if she caught me on the phone again. Covering the volume button on the house phone, I would dial his number and wait for him or his mother to answer the phone. The secrecy we had built had my adrenaline rolling, and I had loved every moment of it… until now.

"I don't know!" I shouted and fled upstairs. Maxwell followed me and sat beside me as I buried my face into my blanket. *Why is this happening to me?* Fear rushed through my body and flooded my mind with the worst possible outcomes. I was scared that my mom would lose custody of me and my sister, and that she would be in trouble for what happened to me. She had been working long, hard hours to provide for us, and I didn't want to jeopardize anything for her.

Then I started questioning my memory. Maybe it wasn't rape. Maybe it was my fault. I had told him to stop, but I didn't really know what was going on in the first place. I could have pushed him off of me, but I had only meekly asked him to stop. And he just kept going, inching his way inside of me as I lay there in agony.

It wasn't like the love scenes in the movies that I would sneak around to watch. Sure, we engaged in the physical act like they did in the movies, but it wasn't romantic or special. The confusing part for me though, was that it wasn't the terrifying kind of rape experience that I had heard about or seen in scary movies. So, maybe it wasn't rape. It was my fault for telling him that I was older. Maybe if I would have told him my real age, he wouldn't have been so interested in me.

I wrestled with these thoughts and with the aftermath. He had stopped answering when I called. He had even stopped saying hi to me and would speak to other girls at church instead of me. Feeling betrayed and conflicted all at once, I embraced the rage that had been boiling up beneath the surface—

"Mani, I am so sorry, but I had to tell them, baby." My stepsister's voice interrupted my cluttered thoughts. "You are only just a baby, and if he hurt you, you need to speak up about it."

I didn't even want to look at her. She was the reason behind all of this! I couldn't trust anyone. She had overheard me while I was on the phone with my crush that night, and then she ran to tell her mom. The next day, I was summoned to my dad's room to talk about what had been reported. And here we were. I glared at my stepsister, upset that she had shared my secret. My sister and I had one more day before we were to go back to our mom's house, and for the first time, I preferred to be there instead of at my dad's.

"I don't want them to take us from mom and send us to some stupid CPS place," I cried, as I lowered my head to my knees, bringing my legs close to my chest. I wanted nothing more at that moment than to find a cave and never leave it. I would supply the cave with a large amount of food, a blanket, and a TV, so that Maxwell and I could watch *The Hills*. If only I could swap lives with one of those characters, or maybe The Kardashians—anyone with a better life than mine.

"But you girls will be able to live here! Isn't that what you want? Either way, you have to speak up if you were raped, baby."

Living in Plano in a large five-bedroom home instead of our 900 square foot, three bedroom apartment sounded promising. I would get to live with our dogs—Maxwell, Sadie, Stinky, and Piggy—instead of sneaking abused cats into my bedroom closet, and I would finally get to be in close proximity to my dad, instead of screaming for him whenever I was being punished by my mom. It really did sound promising.

I DIDN'T UNDERSTAND. Why would he go the extra mile to tell my mom he was fighting for custody if he didn't plan to actually go through with it? My sister Naja and I rode quietly in the backseat, as our mom drove. The silence was thick. This rarely happened in Mom's car, as she always had her favorite radio station playing while we bickered with her, trying to get her to change the station. The tires roared loudly on the pavement until one of us had the audacity to speak.

"Momma, where are we going?" Naja boldly asked.

Looking out the window, I tried to identify any familiar landmarks but found none. We pulled up to a large, intimidating building. I stared at my mom's face in the rearview mirror, waiting for her to answer Naja's question.

"Well, your dad thinks that you girls don't belong to him, so you both are going to take a DNA test." She murmured a few insults under her breath before continuing. "Now, I want you both to know that this is his silly ass mess and not my doing. One day you will know who your heavenly Father is, and He will be much better than the one you have here on earth. Now, come on, girls. It's time to go in."

My heart sank to the floor. *A DNA test? Why would he even think that we weren't his?* We walked into the lobby, and I grabbed one of the lollipops from the receptionist's desk before sitting down. The lollipop certainly couldn't heal the damage that had been done in my heart, but at least it would distract me from listening to my thoughts. I watched my mom as she angrily filled out the paperwork. Naja stood up, pacing around the small lobby before they called us into the room.

We urinated in cups, and the nurses swabbed our mouths. I felt like an animal being tested for an experiment. I didn't feel like a little girl who was loved, cherished, or protected by her dad. We completed everything within twenty minutes, and then we were out the door. On our way home, our mom got us snow cones in an attempt to treat our broken hearts.

"Jackie, I know. I am tired of dealing with his silly ass," she yelled into her phone as we pulled into our apartment parking lot. "These girls don't know what it's like to have a real father. Homer didn't do this to us. He was such a good daddy to us." As she continued her conversation with our Aunt Jackie, Naja and I whispered to each other in the back.

"Why do you try to stand up for him?" Naja scolded me. "It's like you really want to be a daddy's girl. Well, it's not going to happen with him, I can tell you that." She had been hurt the most, since it had been said that our dad was questioning her more than myself. We had similar faces and genetic makeup, but for some reason he was concerned that Naja wasn't his. Being the older sister, I wanted to guard her feelings and confront our dad, but a piece of my heart was still longing for my father to pick up his slack and prove everyone wrong.

"He isn't perfect," I replied, "I just hope that one day he gets it." I knew deep down that this desire would be disappointed. I just hadn't realized that the desire would soon be drowned out by the toxic substances and people I would turn to, to fill the void in my heart.

Tick, tock, tick, tock.

The pendulum of the pink clock on the living room wall resembled my thoughts as they swung back and forth between "he loves me, he loves me not". The sun had fallen asleep, leaving me in the dark room by myself. My sister had chosen to go to bed earlier, and after our somewhat heated discussion about our dad, I wanted to be alone. It had been a rough day. Why couldn't my dad just love us the way my friends' dads loved them?

Tick, tock, tick, tock.

Why did my parents have to do it backwards? Their story was not a love story, nor was there ever a marriage, but there were two babies who would have to witness their hatred towards one another. My sister and I were caught in the middle each time, dealing with the repercussions of a broken home.

"GIRL, YOU HAVE TO BE the most hated chick in high school if you made the Huge Hoes profile picture!" Hope scoffed as she handed me her phone. "That is wild. You aren't even out there like that. They should have put someone else as the profile pic, not you."

We were in the cheerleader locker room at our high school, finishing up with a pep rally, when the page went viral. Everyone in our school and the entire district was well aware that I had made the profile picture. Other girls, including Hope, had been listed on the page with a brief explanation of why they were considered to be a hoe. But I had made the profile picture. I stared at my picture next to the title "Huge Hoes". *At least my picture is cute. Haters.*

"This is so extra," I exclaimed, tossing the phone back to Hope. "Why do I feel like it's one of the seniors on our cheer team? None of them like me. They just hate that I'm a freshman and the senior boys want me. Well, they can come catch these hands if they come at me stupid. When I find out who did it, I will beat their ass." The semester had already been tough enough, with several girls talking about me. I disliked the drama, but I never backed down from an altercation. I was always on defense, and fighting was the mechanism I used to release all my anger.

I stood up to stretch before the basketball game started. I always received a lot of attention at the basketball and football games, and I loved it. The short skirt against my long legs would constantly draw the attention I longed for. Whether the attention was good or bad, it fueled my ego and filled a particular void within me. Of course I always got negative attention from other girls, but I chose to identify that as hate, which only fed my need to compete. If I was being honest with myself, it hurt to feel misunderstood, but I refused to admit that to myself or anyone else. Instead, I tossed the pain of rejection from the Huge Hoes page to the side, allowing it to become fuel to my fire.

"YOU SNUCK INTO A STRIP CLUB?"

"How?"

"What was it like?"

A few of the cheerleaders sat around me barraging me with questions as I shared my experience with them. Some girls scrutinized me, while others were fascinated. It was our sophomore year, and I had received an epiphany that would eventually lead me down a dark road: with the exception of cheerleaders wearing clothes and strippers getting paid, strippers and cheerleaders were basically the same thing! We both danced around in front of people, and the boys at school responded to us the same way guys responded to strippers at the club.

I just had to get up close and personal to see what a strip club was like for myself. Using a fake ID, I got my first taste. There were several stages, and each stage had a woman on it. None of the ladies really smiled; some looked super focused, while others seemed zoned out. There were drinks at our table, and because my ID said that I was 25, I was able to drink.

Though I had shared a lot of what I had experienced at the club with the other cheerleaders, I didn't tell them about my lap dance. It was the first time that I had been so close to another woman. Her scent was so enticing. As she danced on me, I had flashbacks of myself at thirteen, engaging in lesbian pornography—my shameful secret. An urge arose within me to touch her, but I told myself to keep my hands to myself. I often made fun of women who identified themselves as a lesbian, so there was no way that I could have this issue. My mom would kill me, and so many people would judge me. Yet, a seed that had been planted at a young age was just beginning to be watered.

"WADE, TURN TO THE LEFT NOW." The camera snapped as the police officer took my mugshot. "And face forward now."

After I finished with my mugshot, I followed the officer to the desk for fingerprints. My three friends joined her, waiting for their mugshots to be taken. The night had gone horribly wrong. We had initially just wanted to confront Jax for stealing Roxy's money, but a fight broke out, leaving Jax's apartment vandalized and police sirens to follow. A felony? All of my dreams started to shatter, but I shrugged it off, trying to keep my high from the pill I had taken earlier that day. But the questions in my mind were unrelenting. *What would my mom say?*

It had been six months since graduation, and I was living independently as an adult. I had moved out of my mom's house and across the city, with the intention to grow up and "glow up". Attending university was initially ideal for me, but that prospect was immediately ruined during my senior year of high school, when due to my "reckless" behavior, I was sent to a behavioral correction school. Unfortunately, the drugs I was taking at that time didn't provide me with any confidence that I could possibly excel in college, so whatever. I had a plan to snag a wealthy ball player anyway. Then I would meet my life goals. In the meantime, my circle and I all became strippers, working at the same clubs to get money to pay the bills. It made sense, since we did everything together, but I soon discovered that that was actually part of the problem.

"Do you think this is the *Bad Girls Club* or something? You think you're on reality TV, not giving a damn about your future?" The black female officer challenged me with these questions. Ironically enough, I had once desired to be a reality star on *The Bad Girls Club*, but at that particular point in time, I was starting to realize that I did not want that as my reality.

IT WAS CHRISTMAS EVE, and I was still incarcerated. It had been three days, and I was fully sober now. My other friends had been bailed out the first two days, leaving me alone in the cell. Crying quietly on the phone, I called my mom. She encouraged me to pray and just say the name of Jesus, but I was afraid that Jesus would be mad at me. There was no way that He could possibly want to talk to me. I was sure that He hated me. Lying on the hard jail bed, I cried, releasing my frustrations through my tears. My future was ruined.

It had been a long time since I had wept wildly all night. Every time I thought about the loss of my plans or my tarnished reputation, a fresh wave of tears would flow. It didn't help that I didn't have access to tissue. With my face hurting from the strain of crying, I used my prison clothes to wipe my tears.

Exhausted, I curled up on the bed and began to whisper, "Jesus. Jesus. Jesus. Jesus." As I repeated His name, my mind and body finally began to relax, and I drifted off to sleep. Suddenly, a rush of heat fell upon me. Immediately, I sat up. The cell had just been freezing, how was it suddenly so hot? My forehead dripping in sweat, I began to say the name Jesus again, and for the first time, I realized that I was feeling the presence of God. I recalled a faint memory of my mom telling me that His presence would bring me peace. I needed peace in that moment like I had never needed it before. Falling to my knees, I cried out to God.

"I promise I will stop fighting, Lord. It isn't worth it. I'm so sorry I wasted my life making mistakes and following the crowd. Please forgive me." I didn't know what to pray, but I meant what I said to the Lord, and that is all that mattered. As I shut my eyes, the anxiety ceased, and I relaxed.

Then He spoke. *You will be taken care of, my child. Your mistakes are erased.*

My body stayed warmed that night as I held onto the presence of the Lord and the peace that He had brought to me.

Chapter 3
BECOMING HIS

"Imani, I have to tell you something, but I need you to be strong for me, baby. You have to be strong for me." My dad articulated his words slowly, as if each word was painful to say. But nothing could have been more painful than the words that followed. "I have cancer."

Smoke spewed from my lungs, as though I had been punched in the gut. I quickly gathered myself together and took a long, deep breath. It had been almost a year since I had graduated from high school. It had also been a year since I had seen or spoken to my dad. My feelings had been hurt when he hadn't shown up for my high school graduation, but those feelings immediately became irrelevant upon hearing the potential of losing him to cancer.

It just didn't make sense to me. He had always been incredibly healthy; one of the healthiest humans that I knew. This had to be some sick joke or a mistake made by an incompetent doctor who had no business diagnosing people with such terrible diseases. I paced around my apartment, my dog Daisee right at my feet.

"Are you sure?" I asked anxiously. "What kind of cancer?" Hands trembling, I set my bong down on the table.

"I have kidney cancer, but I am going to kick its ass. Your dad will kick its ass," he said firmly.

Thoughts of death were already flooding my mind, but he had said that he was prepared to fight, and that was where my focus needed to be. Using his declaration as a lifeline, I held tightly onto each word and calmed my heart, silently counting to ten and refusing to cry.

"You have to," I responded, "you're supposed to be superman, Dad. If you need some edibles to ease the pain, I can help you with that. I have a connection." I didn't know any other way to help him. I just knew that I wanted to help. He would need encouragement and support during this battle, so all of my issues with him were going to have to move to the side.

"No, I won't be needing that anytime soon," he laughed, "but I do need you to start praying, okay? I need you to pray for me, because a lot of people are doubting that God can heal me. I need your faith and prayers during this time, and for you to stay strong with me."

My dad needed me to pray. He needed my support. He needed my encouragement. He needed me, his daughter.

"I can do that, and I will do that. In the meantime, if anyone says something negative, ignore them. We are going to kick cancer's ass." I wiped tears from my face, scared of what was to come, but happy that for the first time ever, I was going to fight alongside my dad instead of with him.

HILLSONG WORSHIP MUSIC played faintly in the background as I lay on my bed with my journal to my chest and my Bible open next to me. I had just finished writing down the words that I had been believing so faithfully to hear: he beat cancer! Lying there with my heart so full of love and gratitude, I knew that I could trust God. He had cured my father and brought us back to speaking terms.

Several months had passed since Dad had beat cancer, and I had just started going back to church. When I was younger, my mom used to force us to go to church, and I would secretly despise it, but now I actually wanted to go for myself. My heart was finally open to desiring a relationship with Jesus, and I could feel God for the first time in my life. I knew He was with me, yet for some reason He still felt so far from me. Staring at my ceiling, I wondered how I could break through the ceiling in my life in order to experience a deeper relationship with God.

"Hey, girl, what's going on? Is everything okay?" Brie asked, as she answered her phone. She was one of two friends I had that were not in the strip club, and because she was also pursuing change in her own life, I needed to talk to her.

"My dad is healed from cancer, and I know God wants me to stop stripping, but I'm just scared that I won't have it to fall back on, you know? Like, what if I get evicted, become homeless, or I don't make enough money to take care of my needs, you know?" I rambled on and on, going through all of the "what if" scenarios I could fathom. Brie patiently listened before responding.

"Look, all I know is that God healed your dad and brought him back into your life. That is huge. He has your back, so if you want to do something for Him and stop stripping, do it. Don't let anyone stop you from walking out on faith. Plus, you are working at Burberry, right? You can continue there until other doors open." I took a few deep breaths before lighting up my bowl.

"Girl, this is giving me anxiety, but I am going to do it. I just need to trust that you're right."

It didn't take long for a hatred of stripping to come over me. I hated going back to the club. I hated consuming so much alcohol to get Layna to come out of me. I hated having to work even though I had been feeling sick. I hated it more than ever before. Stripping was causing distance between me and Jesus, and I knew it. Thoughts of Jesus returning to Earth while I just so happened to be giving a lap dance bombarded my mind. If that actually were to happen, I wouldn't even know what to say… "I'm sorry, Jesus?" I didn't even want to deal with the possibility. I just wanted to grow closer to Him.

I reached for my Bible and asked God to point me to a verse that confirmed what I needed to do. Randomly, I opened my Bible, and the exact verse that I needed stood out.

Trust in the Lord with all your heart, and lean not on your own understanding; in all your ways submit to Him, and He will make your paths straight.

Proverbs 3:5-6

Tears formed in the corner of my eyes, followed by a sense of joy and peace. I was going to do it. I closed my eyes and told God that I was going to quit dancing. I wanted to give my life to Him. I didn't know what all of it would entail, but if it involved seeing restoration in my life, I wanted every piece of it. I wanted every piece of Jesus.

THE SANTORINI SUN beamed on my shoulders and cheeks, as I sat on the black volcanic sand near the ocean. The waves gently retreated back into the massive sea, before roaring back to me near the shore. *Wow. What an incredible, artistic, and faithful God.*

As a thirteen-year-old girl, full of expectations and dreams, the moment I watched *Sisterhood of the Traveling Pants*, I knew that one day I was going to visit Greece. Sitting on the floor near the television, I dreamed of the day that I would be amongst the beautiful, dreamy, white buildings in Santorini. Ten years later, that thirteen-year-old girl's excitement and curiosity was renewed in my heart.

"God, I will totally move here," I said the first day I arrived. "You just send me, and I won't even ask you twice." Getting there had required a ton of faith, but God had delivered on His promise, as a good Father always does. He provided the funds, support, and the women to travel with for a writer's retreat. My heart was so full.

"Thank you, Abba," I whispered, as I looked up to the blue sky, feeling the presence of the Holy Spirit with me. It had been three years since my dad had become cancer free and I had given my life fully to Jesus. I smiled, loving every minute with God, knowing that He would always have my back. I grabbed my journal and began to jot down what the Holy Spirit was saying to me.

It was my last day in Santorini for the retreat, but I knew that God would bring me back to this magnificent island. I knew that God had other adventures planned for me with plenty of other countries, cultures, and cities that He wanted to show me. I knew that God was always going to be there with me, providing for, loving, and transforming me as I stayed close to Him. I stayed still for another moment, my feet sinking into the sand.

"You will be back, I promise," the reassuring voice of the Holy Spirit whispered to my heart, "and I have so much more that I want to show you, my baby girl."

"IMANI, ARE YOU REALLY USING WISDOM with this decision?" my mother asked. "God is full of wisdom, and this doesn't sound like you heard Him right."

I had just informed her that God had told me to quit my job as a leasing consultant. I had already been down this road three years before, when I had quit stripping, so this was pretty familiar territory for me.

"Well, Mom, I know His voice pretty well, and I already quit. My last day was yesterday, actually." I paused, waiting for either a deep sigh or a barrage of questions. She sighed.

"Well, what are you going to do, Imani? You just got back from Greece, and now you don't have a job."

"Yup. I quit my job because God told me to, and went on a trip to Greece that He sent me on. Sounds crazy, right? I don't know what I'm going to do, but I do know that I heard Him." I also knew that I needed to get off of the phone with her. Her doubts were beginning to cause me to question whether or not I had made the right decision, and I needed to stand on my faith more than ever.

The last time I had quit anything this major for Jesus was when I quit stripping. And God had provided instantly, the following day, when a stranger blessed me with $1,500 for rent. If God had done it for me then, I knew He would deliver on

His promise to me again. I just needed to have faith.

TWO MONTHS HAD PASSED without me working, and it was beginning to test my patience, my faith, and my belief that I had heard God correctly. I was doing everything right! My lifestyle consisted of praying, praising God, going to church, watching my mouth, working a part-time job, and being productive. *What was I missing? Why weren't clients coming to me? Why was it so hard?* Some of my friends were praying for me, and some had even offered to help me out as I walked out on faith. I was incredibly grateful for their support, but where was God?

It was a sunny day after church, and the words Christina had spoken as she had prayed with me were on repeat. "Be real with God. Tell Him how you feel, girl. If it sucks, tell Him! If you are upset, share that with God. You have to be real with Him."

I was in my bedroom, journal in hand, ready to be real with God as she had advised. But how could I tell God that I was disappointed because He wasn't coming through on His promise? Even though I felt like it was daring to let it all out, I went for it anyway.

"God, I am so mad!" I shouted, as I began pacing back and forth in my room. "You have me out here looking crazy, telling people that I stopped working for you! Where are you? Yes, you got me to Greece, but what now? I am doing my part, but I need you to come through, Man, because this is not fun anymore. This sucks. Bill collectors are calling, and I am trying to be a good Christian, but I am on the cusp of cussing out the next person that calls to ask me for money!" Falling to my knees with tears racing down my cheeks, I stuttered between sighs and sobs, "This is NOT what I signed up for. Where are you?"

"I'm here," His gentle voice replied, "I just needed you to be honest with your feelings. I needed you to take away the fake smile, and tell me how you really feel. I will tell you what to do next." The Holy Spirit rushed into the room, filling my mind and heart with His presence. I felt as if someone wearing a fuzzy warm sweater was giving me a hug.

All my life, I had been keeping my emotions in, only to release them through fighting, sex, drugs, or anything other destructive activity I could find. But God was trying to teach me that I could keep it real with Him and share my emotions in a safe space. Apparently, He had some issues He needed to address in my heart before He could fulfill His promise to me.

"I GOT THE JOB!" I screamed, with my sister in the car. We were heading back home from getting groceries with a food stamp card a friend had allowed me to borrow. It had been a long yet rewarding summer of believing God's word. I took my phone off of mute after we finished screaming, so that we could hear what the recruiter was saying.

"You know, it's actually good that you aren't working at your former job anymore, because they are a client of ours. If you were still working there, I would have had to contact your regional manager prior to interviewing you for permission, because we would technically be stealing their employee. So, it's great that you ended up leaving. It makes things a lot easier on my end." She finished up the conversation by telling me the salary amount. Once she hung up the phone, my sister and I looked at each other and screamed with joy again.

My salary had doubled from what I was making at my previous job. I punched the air, and we continued shouting for five minutes straight. We hugged each other, high-fived, and thanked God through tears. He had come through DOUBLE what I had anticipated, and I had scored a job for which I had no degree or credentials. Through all I had been through, God knew what He had planned for me; plans to help me, not to harm me. And all the while, He kept loving and pursuing this former bad girl who was undeserving, but oh, so thankful for His mercy and grace.

A Letter from Me to You

Dear Loved One,

You are indeed loved; like, REALLY loved. God loves you. You are heard. You are seen. You are remembered. And if you can't remember anything else, or if you aren't ready to emotionally handle anything else, just hold on to that truth. You are loved.

When I initially went back to Jesus, I thought I was too dirty. Maybe you can relate. Or maybe you are following Jesus, but you are bored, restless, or still believing God for restoration in a particular area of your life—whether it is finances, relationships with parents, your marriage, your health, your family, or your identity—but you haven't seen anything yet. I can understand that, too.

Even though God has begun the process of restoring my relationship with both of my parents, I am still believing God for restoration in other areas of my life. If we are being honest here, you and I both know that trusting God when you can't see any immediate results is hard! But God is not a liar, and if He said He will do it, then He will.

Perhaps the previous three chapters caused you to reflect on your own story. Are you happy with the way your life has unfolded? I know I'm not. I would have rather had the perfect story, free of pain and bad decisions. Girl, I wish. But here is the good news for us: God is the one writing our story, and He is the greatest storyteller there is. All you have to do is give your life to Jesus, accept Him into your heart, and pursue Him intentionally.

Although I have been through things that God never wanted me to experience, He has and will continue to use my story to reach many women, and He will heal me. And in the end, it will all be for His glory and it will help to advance His kingdom. Wouldn't you want to be part of something so much bigger than yourself? Advance the kingdom of God by allowing Him to open your eyes to see how He has written your story.

And you don't have to do it alone. I want us to lock arms, share with each other, heal, and become more like Jesus together. If you haven't accepted Him into your life yet, and you are wondering how to do this, I want you to know that you do not have to be perfect to come to Him. I was attending church for months before I finally stopped stripping.

But let me interject here that I don't share that as if to say, "Yeah, girl, keep on doin' ya thang. God has grace for you." Yes, He does offer grace, but I was confused at that time, and there's a difference between not knowing any better and knowing exactly what you're doing and taking advantage of God's grace.

When God showed up in my life, I no longer wanted to strip, and I eventually stopped smoking because I knew that it had become an idol to me and a hindrance in my relationship with Jesus. He's the one who did the transformation in me. I just said "Yes". So, I will say it again, you do not have to come as a perfect person, just as someone desiring an authentic, life changing relationship with Jesus.

If you are ready to make that decision right now, just open your heart and say the following words aloud:

> *Lord Jesus, I ask for you to come into my heart and make it your residence. I accept you as my Lord and Savior. Help me to trust you, no matter what comes my way, and allow me to experience all of who you are. Help me to surrender concerns, idols, and anything else that seeks to stand in the way of relationship with you. Help me to love you deeply and to love learning more about you. Thank you for inviting me into this relationship with you and for loving me. I love you, Lord, and I ask all of these things in Jesus's name. Amen.*

Now, get ready for God to do more work in you as you become who He has called you to be. I am excited for you, I am praying for you, and I love you!

Sincerely,

Imani Wade

Chapter 4
BLASTS FROM YOUR PAST

Each day of our lives is packed with tons of lessons. While some of these lessons are simple and practical, like taking your contacts out before you go to sleep or cleansing your face before you go to bed, other lessons can be intense. These are the lessons that require you to trust God on a whole new level. Sometimes they are lessons you have to learn as the result of a horrible decision that you made, and sometimes they are lessons that you thought you had passed, only to have the demons of your past taunting you. In this chapter, I want to focus on *those* kinds of lessons.

There are times that we wish that God would just click the "delete" button on our past so that all of our flaws, bad decisions, and messy mistakes would disappear. Another way I've heard it put is to "leave your past in the past". But that's not how God works. When we follow Jesus, He makes us into a new person in Christ and gives us a new identity in Him; one that He designed long before we were even born.

Then Jesus said to his disciples, 'Whoever wants to be my disciple must deny themselves and take up their cross and follow me. For whoever wants to save their life will lose it, but whoever loses their life for me will find it.'

- Matthew 16:24-25

Therefore, if anyone is in Christ, the new creation has come: The old has gone, the new is here!

- 2 Corinthians 5:17

If the Word of God says that you and I have a new identity in Christ, then why do we still get blasted by battles from our past? I know that I am not the only one who has overcome a struggle only to find myself crying or screaming when the same test, temptation, or trigger returns. Here's the reality that we have to face: though you and I are new creations in Christ, we still have a past that is part of our story. Navigating your future when your past keeps trying to remind you of who you used to be or what has happened to you can be tricky.

For instance, what are you supposed to do when you have scary dreams or flashbacks that begin to haunt you? How do you keep yourself from rejecting a good man of God when you have trust issues from previous relationships? What happens when you're faced with disappointment, betrayal or rejection, and that destructive habit you used to rely on for comfort returns?

You see, no matter how much we may want to leave our past in the past, it is impossible—especially if we desire true inner healing. As great as it may sound to be able to forget your past, what you're really doing is numbing yourself and glossing over all of the deep matters of the heart that God wants to walk through with you.

Now, I want to be clear. Wallowing in your past or revisiting certain people or habits from your past is foolish. That may sound harsh, but I say this harshly only because I can. I've been there myself, plenty of times. I've called my ex-girlfriend numerous times, tried to rekindle friendships with people God wanted me to release, and I've held onto destructive mindsets connected to my past. Trust me, if you aren't careful with revisiting your past, the whole experience can feel like pouring salt onto an open wound.

But revisiting your past in order to grieve, heal, and grow is both wise and brave. Recalling a nasty divorce, a rape, a breakup, a disappointment, a death, or any other painful situation is not only challenging, but it hurts. It takes strength to go back to that place and allow yourself to feel those emotions in order to heal from them. As my favorite teacher Lysa Terkeurst says, "You have to feel it to free it."

So how do we overcome these struggles so we can walk in our new identities? We do so by fighting. Freedom is ours, but we have to fight to remind ourselves who we really are. This is a fight that requires digging into the Word of God, standing on His truth, and allowing Him to invade our space. We must swallow the Word of God daily, because it is literally medicine to our wounds. All of this is necessary if we expect to be able to fight the temptations, triggers, and tests that come our way.

Of course, there will be moments when we will feel like we cannot fight anymore, and we're allowed to feel that way, but that is when we have to lean on God most and open up to Him about our struggles. He already knows about them; He just wants us to *want* to talk to Him about them, which requires being humble enough to admit that we do not have it all figured it out and that we need God's strength. Otherwise, we are slaves to our old sinful nature. And that is NO way to live a new life in Christ!

It is for freedom that Christ has set us free. Stand firm, then, and do not let yourselves be burdened again by a yoke of slavery.

- Galatians 5:1

So if the Son sets you free, you will be free indeed.

- John 8:36

Let us not become weary in doing good, for at the proper time we will reap a harvest if we do not give up.

- Galatians 6:9

Diving into the depths of our past will look different for each of us. This is where you have to decide with God what revisiting your past in pursuit of your healing entails. For some people, healing comes through quiet time with the Lord or with a

Christian counselor who can partner with you for your healing. For others of us, it is through writing about our story or sharing our story more openly.

When I tell you that I did NOT want anyone to know that I was a former stripper, drug addict, bi-sexual, belligerent, daddy issue-having girl, you better believe I did NOT! And that went especially for church folks. I wanted to fit in. I didn't want to be a misfit, judged, or even victimized. And like some of you reading this right now, I also had a ton of shame attached to my story. But this is the path that God has led me down, and I'm finding healing through writing about my story, opening up with trusted loved ones, and by being real with God regarding my emotions.

Part of the perfectionist façade I mentioned struggling with in the introduction of this book meant that I wasn't just faking it in front of other people; I was faking it in front of God by pretending that everything was fine as I prayed very generic prayers. God just simply wants me to KEEP IT REAL. I am still a work in progress, but I am learning to be bold and fearless with sharing these feelings with God. I am learning how to love the lessons of life, and to live within them.

Maybe your story isn't the same as my own, but I know that you can relate to some of the mental challenges and pains that I once faced. Whether or not you can say "Yup, I have been a stripper too, girl, I get it!" you may understand what it feels like to crave control of your life and other people. Or maybe you may understand feeling trapped, unworthy, belittled, and abandoned.

It is my hope that some of the lessons I share here may end up blessing you or bringing that "aha" moment that you are seeking. Or maybe by sharing my story, you will be encouraged to share yours. Your story is your story, and the lessons you have learned will not only help you, but also many other people, if you decide to share them. Your story will be used for God's glory, if you allow Him to use it.

So, alas, here I am today, sharing my story with you. I pray that as we walk through this book together, you continue to heal, grow, and fall in love with your own journey and the lessons you are learning along the way. And while I desire that you have moments where you can relate to my story, I deeply desire for us both to get more connected with God as we continue our journey into becoming the women He has called us to be.

Chapter Four Reflections

1. What lessons have you learned that are currently shaping the way you live your life?

_____

_____

_____

_____

_____

2. Is there anything from your past that triggers you to remember these lessons?

_____

_____

_____

_____

_____

_____

3. How do you typically respond with these blast from the past battles? Is it a harmful or helpful response?

4. Have you shared your story with non-believers and other Christians? If so, which group do you find it is easier to share your story with and why? If not, why not?

5. Revisiting your past to grieve, heal, and grow, is both wise and brave. Do you believe that you have done this? If not, why not?

_____

_____

_____

_____

_____

6. Ask God what your journey of healing entails. Does it involve sharing your story with a trusted friend or your church community? Write down what the Lord reveals.

_____

_____

_____

_____

_____

Chapter 5
BREAKING UP WITH THE BAD GIRL

I recently had to break up with the bad girl.
"Break up with the bad girl?" you're probably wondering, "do you mean as in dating?"

No, the bad girl that I'm referring to is the persona that I developed after being raped at the age of 12. I'm talking about the bad girl who made it okay for me to be in the strip club, to go to parties, to act out in anger, to engage in homosexuality, and to develop a drug addiction.

That bad girl.

The bad girl image is heavily promoted in today's media through shows like *Bad Girls Club* and songs like "Bad Girl" by Wale, just to name a few. Modern media portrays being a bad girl as what is hot, trendy or cute, but in all actuality, the bad girl is really a heartbroken little girl hiding behind her pain and masking it with activities that "feel good" in the moment. She's running from healing and wholeness by pretending to be someone that she isn't.

Being a bad girl is a mindset that is created as a defense mechanism to protect us from the hurt we have experienced in our life. So, yes, even if you were raised in the church and kept your virginity up until marriage, you can still obtain the bad girl status. We all have felt rejection, desire for control, insecurity, lust, anger, and pain to some degree, and those are the exact entry points the bad girl needs to take over our lives.

So, yes, I HAD to break up with her. But I had been with her for so long, that I didn't know how to live without her. She was no longer just a mindset for me, but she had become my way of LIVING.

How was I going to develop healthy relationships with the women God had put in my life, when I had so many trust issues?

How was I supposed to remain pure, when I had lived a promiscuous lifestyle for a huge portion of my life?

How could I pray prayers focused on releasing myself from strongholds and chains, if I was repeating the same toxic habits?

While I was witnessing victory in certain areas of my life, I still found myself coming face to face with the same struggles—all of which were connected to the bad girl mindset.

She had to go.

AS I LAY OUT ON MY RUG, journal to my chest, and tears flowing down my cheeks, I couldn't help but to feel like a failure. Sexually sinning AGAIN? Had I not already gone through the process of confessing, repenting, crying, and then telling my friend so that I had accountability? My goodness, why could I not get it together?

Making good on my promise to God to stop fighting was easy. One trip to jail and an encounter with God was enough to make me keep my hands to myself. As soon as I had gotten home, I threw away the brass knuckles, knives, and everything else that was associated with that lifestyle (ratchet, I know).

Done.

It was also easy to stop smoking weed, especially since I had thrown away the bongs and everything else that came with that lifestyle.

Done.

Once my heart was sold out for God, it was even easy for me to stop stripping—even with no way to pay rent. I had stepped out on faith, and the lingerie, shoes, and fake hair were tossed out. I threw away everything that came with that lifestyle.

Done.

But why was I struggling with remaining pure? I had spent three years being celibate, really trying to honor my body and the Holy Spirit.

Then, BOOM, I had sex.

One year later, I had gotten close to God again. I was growing, and He was being so faithful to me.

Then, BOOM, I had sex again, slapping God right in the face with my broken promises.

She had to go.

Lying there on the floor crying, I heard the Holy Spirit prompt me to go for a quick stroll outside. As I walked around my apartment building, I heard the words, "You have no value; I'm breaking up with you." This moment would eventually lead me to write a song and a letter called "Breaking Up with the Bad Girl".

One of these days, I intend to share the song with you; however, I want to share the letter now, as I truly believe that it can help you decide if you need to break up with the bad girl. Please don't skip over it because it is in italics (I know that's what I usually do that when I read books, ha).

A Letter to the Bad Girl

Why are you so mad? Okay, I'm direct, yes, but I promise I want nothing from you, even though everyone else always seems to want a piece of you—if not all of you. I know what you are going through, though I cannot possibly fathom every emotion you are feeling. Or did you block all of that out? The ability to feel love, sadness, and loneliness—have you blocked all of that out of your heart? I had. I didn't want anyone to know if or when they had hurt me, so most of the time I would keep my composure. There were a few times that I lashed out on people, but only because rage was the only emotion that made sense to combat the pain.

I know, girl, everyone wants to call themselves by your name, but do they know what comes with this lifestyle? Do they know about the empty moments you feel or about the way you have to suppress every bit of self-expression that wants to come out of you? Do they know that you hide behind a smile or a smirk because you have to pretend to be someone that you're not?

What happened to the younger you? You know, the sweet little girl who used to run free and laugh loudly. What happened to the girl who used to dream fearlessly and love wholly? Who hurt her first? Who disappointed her first? Who rejected her, leaving her to feel empty and worthless?

Was it the crush she had in elementary school who insulted her in front of the entire third grade?

Was it the friend who kissed her crush?

Could it have been the dad who never called or answered her call, leaving her to feel abandoned?

Or was it her mom who was more concerned about men than her wellbeing?

Maybe it was the person who molested her and robbed her of her innocence and trust.

Or was it the teacher who called her stupid and insisted that she would never amount to anything in life?

You deserve to be mad. You deserved way more, and you got way less.

You know, in light of all of this, I don't think that the name Bad Girl suits you. I mean, looking on the outside, sure, a stranger or those who follow you may disagree with me. They think they know you because they see you consistently posting on Instagram and smiling on Snapchat. Yeah, they think they know you. Everyone says they know you, but nobody really does. You're okay with that though, because it's safe. You're protecting yourself from being betrayed again by people who try to take advantage of you.

And that is why you can have sex yet remain emotionally disconnected. That is why the use of your body as a commodity or trophy feels normal. That is why you have numbed yourself to feeling anything deeper than surface level emotions. That is why you choose to take back all of those shots each weekend or drink an entire bottle of wine when you're all alone. And that is why you pick up the phone to call someone for attention or sex. After all, that's what you have been all your life... an object or tool that's meant to be used.

Hey, Bad Girl? I want to stop calling you that. What is your name? Who are you really? Have you figured that out yet? That's okay, me neither. I am still trying to get my life together. I am still trying to break the destructive habits that try to dismiss my progress and delay my destiny. I am trying, girl, but it is not easy.

We think it's easier being a bad girl—living a detached life and doing whatever we want, whenever we want—but this wild, rebellious life kills us slowly. Years later, we wake up crying, feeling all of the emotions we had spent so long trying not to feel. Alone and hopeless, we find ourselves banging our head against a steering wheel or cursing ourselves because of the self-hatred that had grown in our hearts as we established our bad girl image. We realize that we're lacking real connections with people, because "people suck" and they don't know what to do with our heart or with our real, authentic self. I get it.

I broke up with the bad girl who used to follow me, assuring me that she had my back. I had to break up with her because she was blocking me from knowing myself. I'm still learning about my worth and discovering who I am and whose I am. I know there is someone who deserves me (all of me), although I don't always deserve Him. He designed you and me so uniquely, and His love is so genuine, even when we're a hot mess. I am trying to limit the amount of hot messiness in my life, but it is a journey.

Oh, and guess what? If you aren't ready or don't know how to break up with the bad girl, just bring her with you when you come to God. While He works on you to transform you into His image, it will become increasingly uncomfortable for her to stay. Why? Because His presence is growing inside of you, and where His Spirit is, there is freedom. Trust me, the bad girl won't sit around for long. Just don't go around missing or looking for her though. This new, pure and vibrant you is worth pursuing and fully developing.

I also have good news! The bad girl **can't** stay long, because she doesn't belong to you. She was not there when God created you, nor was she there when you were an innocent and carefree child. She only came along as an alternative to the pain you had pushed away. So, as long as you run to God and keep pursuing your growth, she can't stay. Keep seeking, and you will find your truest self when you find Him.

THIS LETTER WAS ACTUALLY WRITTEN just a month before today (the day I'm writing this chapter), and she has already tried to creep back into my life. For so long, she had ruled over my mind, my habits, and the way I lived my life, so of course she would try to return. But I promised myself and God that I would not allow her to reign over my mind anymore. She cannot come back.

Later in this chapter, I am going to equip you with some action items that can help if she tries to return in your life, but first, let's pause and reflect. How do you know if you're still living with the bad girl? Below, I have listed some of the behaviors and signs that I have noticed within myself that are influenced by the bad girl:

- You keep repeating the same mistakes and repenting about the same things. "As a dog returns to its vomit, so does a fool repeat its folly" (Proverbs 26:11).

- You find yourself responding to people and situations irrationally and immaturely, instead of seeking to understand or seeking God for guidance.

- You pick fights easily and find yourself surrounded by drama. "What is causing the quarrels and fights among you? Don't they come from the evil desires at war within you?" (James 4:1 NLT).

- Anger is your most common emotion, and offense follows you.

- You cannot trust anyone.

- It is typically hard to correct you, because you do not receive correction well. This is a rebellious and prideful mindset that will hinder any growth you desire to make in life. "Pride leads to conflict, but those who take advice are wise" (Proverbs 13:10 NLT).

- You find yourself holding grudges instead of pursuing forgiveness and patience with people. "A wise person demonstrates patience, for mercy means holding your tongue. When you are insulted, be quick to forgive and forget it, for you are virtuous when you overlook an offense" (Proverbs 19:11 TPT).

- You repeat destructive habits that you once had in the past. Every time I wanted to get my dad's attention in high school, I would act out because I knew he would answer my mom's call if I was in trouble. When I got saved, I brought this same mentality to my relationship with God and found myself acting out and sinning because I felt forgotten by my heavenly Father.

- Lack of responsibility for your own decisions. "There are some people who ruin their own lives and then blame it all on God" (Proverbs 19:3 TPT).

- You desire full control of your life, and you find it difficult to submit to God and trust Him with your life. "Trust in the Lord with all of your heart and lean not unto your own understanding. In all your ways, submit to Him, and He will make your paths straight" (Proverbs 3:5-6).

- You crave attention to validate your worth. If you struggle in this area, I suggest taking a two to five month break from social media, as it is one of the biggest methods of seeking attention. "You desire but **do not** have, so you kill. You **covet** but you cannot get what you want, so you quarrel and fight. You **do not have** because you **do not** ask God" (James 4:2).

- You make impulsive decisions rooted in a fear of loss or a fear of missing out.

- You try to rush God with your plans, and the thought of following His process and timing is ridiculous to you!

- You demonstrate obsessive behavior towards friendships or relationships because you fear that they may reject you or abandon you. There was a point and time in my life that I did NOT like sharing friends. I wanted my friends to only need me. This mentality was created when I found out that my dad had remarried and had stepchildren.

- You isolate yourself from community, claiming "God's got me," but in reality, you are afraid of getting hurt.

- You are always thinking about your own interests above others.

- You run from God so you don't have to obey whatever it is that He has called you to do. I ran from writing this book as well as following through on some other things in my life. Eventually, I decided to submit, but that is still delayed obedience. *Read Jonah 1.*

- You feel unqualified and unworthy to be loved by God or to fulfill the dreams He has given you.

- You turn to other substances, activities, or people to numb your pain instead of giving them to God. That includes sex, shopping, busy work, alcohol, talking to your bestie instead of God, binge-watching TV, obsessively working out, and so on. These can become idols, if we are not careful! "Do not turn away to useless idols. They do no good, and they cannot rescue you, because they are useless" (1 Samuel 12:21 TPT).

- You become incredibly impatient with people, lacking compassion for their struggles because their problems aren't as big as yours. I have been guilty of this, and I have learned that all struggles are important and seen by God.

- You cover conceit with confidence. Basically, you think that the universe revolves around you.

- You are unforgiving towards yourself or you get overly angry with yourself when you make mistakes.

- You look up to an alter ego or celebrity or friend and think, "What would _____ do?" instead of inquiring what Jesus would do. Before getting saved, I would think of Rihanna, Kim K., and even my former best friend. I have since grown to ask God for wisdom and for Him to direct me to anyone who might have insight on a matter I am needing clarity on. "If any of you lacks **wisdom,** you should ask God, who gives generously to all without finding fault, and it will be given to you" (James 1:5).

Honestly, this list can go on, but this is a good starting point. So I ask you again, do you need to break up with the bad girl?

While I wish that writing a letter marked the absolute end of this mindset for me, I have to be honest. It wasn't. I always like to say, "You didn't get here overnight, so you won't heal overnight," and that is a tough truth that I am learning to live by. Transformation into the image of Christ is a daily process, a moment-by-moment journey, and a lifelong pursuit. When we become more like Jesus, we will ultimately become the woman He created us to be. But this woman isn't some perfect female in a box, grinning from ear to ear, refusing to acknowledge her mistakes or frustrations.

No, she is real.

She is a real woman with real feelings, living in a very real world with really crazy people in it.

Yet her heart is decided.

Each day, she decides to show up, expecting her Savior to be with her wherever she goes.

When she feels overwhelmed, she lies down and closes her eyes, taking deep breaths as she silences her inner voice to hear His voice.

She has a heart of praise that can't help but to worship God.

She surrounds herself with other healthy believers, being transparent as they love and pray for her.

She writes or talks about how she feels, instead of running from her emotions.

She invites God to shed His light on the darkest places of her heart, allowing Him to fill her up with His love and grace.

She is recognizes her weaknesses and seeks God for strength.

She is focused on learning more about God and who she is in Him.

She is intentional.

You see, there is no room for the bad girl in the Kingdom of God. She has to go. But if she ever returns, just show her the door and ask God to help you handle it.

Chapter Five Reflections

1. Do you need to break up with the bad girl? If not, do you have someone in your close circle that can agree with you?

   _____

   _____

   _____

   _____

   _____

2. Which habits from the bad girl list did you recognize in yourself that you need to seek God's freedom from?

   _____

   _____

   _____

   _____

   _____

3. Reflecting on your past, what do you think brought the bad girl mindset into your life?

_____

_____

_____

_____

_____

4. Is there anyone that you need to forgive?

_____

_____

_____

_____

_____

_____

5. Write a letter breaking up with the bad girl. Then write a letter to God, asking Him for help with this decision.

_____

_____

_____

_____

_____

_____

_____

_____

_____

_____

_____

_____

_____

_____

_____

Chapter 6
THE BAD GIRL BLUES

I feel like I spend a whole lot of time praying that God will shut my mouth and renew my mind to be more like His. How often does this actually work for me, you ask? Only when I apply His correction, and I allow myself to be slow to speak. Let's take today, for instance.

Today, I experienced an annoyance that many of you can probably relate to: terrible customer service. And while I wish I could say that this incident was something that pertained to my internet bill or electricity, it wasn't. It involved something even worse, something more important to me… my food. For the sake of not blasting the company at fault, I will call their business BlashBash.

So, this afternoon, some fellow employees and I had decided that we were craving food from Zoe's Kitchen. We placed our order, and the BlashBash driver agreed to pick it up and deliver it for us. As it turns out, the delivery was delayed by an hour… a WHOLE hour. My hopes for receiving this food in a timely manner had been high (along with my appetite), until I got the message stating that the driver was going to pick up another order before delivering mine.

Excuse me? I screamed in my mind, dreading the thought of cold pita bread. We only had an hour for our lunch break! Anyone else probably would have politely responded with, "That's fine, we can wait," but no, not Imani. Hungry for justice, I engaged in some very intense conversation with the driver (once she finally arrived), and in the end, we received a full refund for all four of our orders.

But what was I really mad about? Was it really the food or did I already have some anger being built up that I needed to explore? Before you roll your eyes, let me explain. Sometimes the way we react to an interruption in our lives has little to do with the interruption itself, but more to do with the intention behind the interruption. Sure, my hunger influenced my response in this particular situation, but I was more upset that the driver had put my needs on pause to fulfill someone else's needs. Moreover, she hadn't kept her word. When I look back now, I can see that my response in that moment was similar to responses I have had in the past towards individuals who didn't respect me or honor my needs.

I wish I could say that this revelation had come to me before I finished eating my pita bread, but nope. Instead, I chose to continue talking about the disservice and praise myself for how I had gotten the refund for everyone.

But at what cost?

The remainder of the day, other difficult circumstances arose, inciting yet another level of annoyance. The seed of bitterness that had been planted in my heart continued to lodge itself deeper, causing my attitude to become more and more bitter.

At least by the time I got home, I repented. While I am grateful for God's grace and the ability to run to the throne to repent, I am tired of repenting about the SAME THINGS…

"Lord, help me keep my mouth shut when people say things that test me."

"Lord, help me to be more like you and take charge of my thoughts."

"God, I'm sorry for having a bad attitude and for making fun of people."

I told you that I am not perfect, and I promised transparency, right? As a former bad girl seeking to become more like Jesus, I know that this transformation is going to be a PROCESS. But that wasn't always the case. At one point, I really did believe that I was going to be made perfect overnight, so I tried my hardest to be just that... perfect.

But perfection doesn't exist on Earth; only in heaven. Jesus was the only human to ever walk this Earth and live a perfect life. So, guess what? That means if we want to achieve perfection, you can only do it with Jesus! Our transformation into becoming like Christ is a process we undergo on a daily basis. It begins the moment you accept Jesus into your heart, and it continues until the day you stand before His throne in heaven. It is a minute-by-minute, breathe in and breathe out pursuit of Jesus. Don't believe me? Let's go over some typical scenarios, as I am sure you can relate to at least one of them.

- You just received an email from a difficult person. You know the Bible says to be slow to speak, quick to listen, and slow to anger (James 1:19), yet here you are huffing and puffing under your breath, possibly even letting a cuss word or two slip.

- Your kids aren't giving you space, and you are so close to booking a one way ticket to someplace far away for a few days—maybe even for the rest of your life.

- You want to appreciate everything that you have, because you are truly blessed, but you find yourself coveting another woman's life.

- You are constantly fighting the urge to text your ex or stalk him on Instagram, but you know if you let him back into your life, destruction will soon follow.

- You had a long week and feel like you deserve a mini shopping spree, mimosas, and a binge session of your favorite show. Why go to God when you can do things that make you feel good instead?

Yes, you understand exactly what I am talking about! I call moments like these in our transformation process the "Bad Girl Blues." These are the types of behaviors that once acted as our defense mechanisms, when the bad girl was in our lives. Anytime that I felt hurt that my dad wasn't answering my calls, the feeling of rejection would drive me to the nearest party. That was just one of the ways I would protect myself. A few other defense mechanisms I often relied on were sex, weed, alcohol, fighting and partying.

    Now, as a Christian woman, the list looks different. Instead of fighting, I find myself verbally or mentally abusing people when they don't value my time or needs. Instead of smoking weed, sometimes I comfort myself by overeating. And instead of having sex, I would fill my desire for attention by flirting; getting attention from men who are not even close to being marriage material. You see? These defense mechanisms stay stuck in our habits, so we have to be intentional about breaking free from them, if we want to become more like Jesus. But how do we do that?

For starters, we need to become more self-aware. So many times we hear a sermon, read a verse, or see a meme and immediately think, "Oh my gosh! This message is for my friend. I need to send this to her!" But if we were more aware about our own transformation process, we would know that the message is really for us.

Nobody knows you better than God, and that is the perfect reason to invite Him into your journey towards becoming more self-aware. I think a lot of times people hear the terms "self-aware" or "self-love", and they want to roll their eyes and dismiss the subject altogether. But while I do believe that God comes first, I also believe that learning about who you are, where you are, and where you are going is *incredibly* important for successful transformation.

Being self-aware helps you understand the way your mind and heart truly work.

Being self-aware helps you identify those moments when you are operating out of fear or reverting back to former defense mechanisms.

Being self-aware helps you review your progress and determine how you can improve.

Being self-aware helps you understand what kind of relationships you need in your life, and which ones you don't need to tolerate anymore.

Being self-aware helps you get closer to God, because you are no longer hiding behind a mask. You can come to Him without being fake.

One of the greatest benefits of being self-aware is that it helps you to be more open to experiencing moments of revelation from the Holy Spirit. He can point you to the exact reasons you respond to situations the way that you do—even if the answer can only be found hidden somewhere in your past.

Recently, God removed three friends from my life. Although it really hurt, I know that He was doing something new in me, and they had served their purpose in my life for a season. That season had ended. Had I let them go when their season was over with in the first place or sought God about the purpose of their role in my life, I could have avoided the heartbreak of having God remove them for me.

When it came to repairing my relationship with my dad, I had expectations that he was not emotionally capable of meeting, and I ended up feeling rejected, once again. However, he really just needed grace, and I really just needed to rely on God as my Father.

Hearing people talk about themselves all the time used to really annoy me. When I'm having a conversation with someone, and they don't ask me any questions about my life, it seems they have little interest in me as a person. While this may be true with some people, I have also realized that situations like this were mainly frustrating for me, because I desired to be heard and affirmed.

Do you see the pattern? Being self-aware allows me to identify if I am listening to lies from the enemy or making assumptions. In each of those instances, I was not trying to hear or see what the Holy Spirit was trying to show me, because I was hurt. It is okay to be hurt, but we can't stay there. Instead of responding to these types of situations with my defense mechanisms, I need to combat the "Bad Girl Blues" in a different way.

When I feel a defense mechanism trying to control my emotions, I need to walk away. Like, literally, walk away. Wherever I am, I need to dismiss myself politely and just step away. Then, I need to breathe. "Abba, Abba, Abba." Breathing the name of God, I call on His strength and grace to carry me through.

Then call on me when you are in trouble, and I will rescue you, and you will give me glory.

- Psalm 50:15 (NLT)

I called to the LORD, who is worthy of praise, and have been saved from my enemies.

- 2 Samuel 22:4

Call to Me and I will answer you and tell you great and unsearchable things you do not know.

- Jeremiah 33:3

Then you will call on Me and come and pray to Me, and I will listen to you. You will seek Me and find Me, when you seek Me with all your heart.

- Jeremiah 29:12-13

Each of these verses use the word "call". So, instead of picking up the phone to call a friend or your parent, call on God. He is your friend, your comforter, and your helper. And in that moment, if we really wait before reacting, we will feel the Holy Spirit fill us up with His peace.

His peace will guide you as you respond to the email from the difficult person.

His peace will strengthen you and bring you joy when you are ready to hit the "runaway" button.

His peace will bring you contentment and teach you how to praise instead of complain when you are struggling with coveting another woman's life.

His peace will embrace you and remind you of how valuable you are, when you are tempted to text or stalk your ex.

His peace can and will do all of this, if we only take the initiative to pursue Him. Run to the throne as a daughter of the Most High King. Take as much time as you need when sitting at His throne. It is your right as His daughter. You belong there. Soak in His glory, cry it out if you need to, write it out if you need to, and give the burden you are carrying to your Father.

God knows all about the "Bad Girl Blues", so you can believe that He knows exactly how to help you break free from them. Your defense mechanisms have to go! My defense mechanisms? Well, yes, they have to go too.

Chapter Six Reflections

1. What are your current Bad Girl Blues? How do you know that these are defense mechanisms?

   _____

   _____

   _____

   _____

   _____

2. List a few activities that you will do by yourself to get to know yourself better (i.e. writing, booking a solo trip, taking a walk, taking a cooking class, etc.). Commit to doing two of these things within the next three months, if possible, and invite Jesus to go with you.

   _____

   _____

   _____

   _____

   _____

3. What can you do when facing the Bad Girl Blues? Strategize with God and list your strategies.

4. How can you become more self-aware? In what ways do you believe it will benefit you?

Chapter 7
MINDSET MAKEOVER

"Nope, that is not who I am anymore, Satan. Try again." I was standing in front of the mirror, getting ready to head out, when I received a text message that would potentially put me in a position to run back to an old mindset. Before responding, I had to take a moment to remind myself (and the enemy) of who I was.

I was no longer a woman who manipulated men for their money, but I had become a woman who encouraged men. The old me needed attention and validation, but the new me was a woman who knew her worth and from whom it came. I knew these things, but Satan was clearly confused about which Imani he was trying to mess with.

The text message from a man I had recently played mind games with (let's just go ahead and say it… a sugar daddy) lingered on my phone. *Ugh*. I knew I should have changed my number, but I hadn't done it yet. To be fair, the man was just saying hi, but still… he had no business being on my phone. He and I both knew that "saying hi" wasn't just small talk, and this wasn't the first time he was reaching out.

Glancing at the text again, I politely reminded the man that I was his daughter's age and advised him to evaluate his motives with Jesus. After that, I deleted his information from my phone and walked out the door, feeling accomplished for overcoming the manipulation mindset once again.

When breaking up with the bad girl, there will be many habits, behaviors, attitudes and mindsets that we will have to let go. In this chapter, I am going to list a few mindsets that I have had to release, as well as some that I still battle with overcoming.

The Scarcity Mindset

This mindset tells me that I will never have enough, and that God has forgotten about me. It is the little voice in my head that whispers, "Why not me?" as it stirs up jealousy and greed in my soul. There were times in my life when I would try to be happy for a friend's success, but I would find myself coveting what she had or competing with her. And if I allowed this mindset's lies to fester in my heart, I would find myself doing everything that I could to make my own happiness instead of trusting that God was going to take care of me.

You can combat this mindset by reminding yourself daily that God has a detailed and prosperous plan for your life. Refer to Jeremiah 29:11 and the whole chapter of John 15.

The Manipulation Mindset

This mindset is really vicious, due to its controlling nature.

Control: you want what YOU want, and you use people to make it happen.

When I was stripping, I would manipulate both genders to get what I wanted—from purses to clothes to money, and even attention. My personal strategy was to learn what a person was like, according to their horoscope, and then I would use that information to get what I wanted.

If this mindset is not addressed and released, it won't be long before you find yourself trying to manipulate God into giving you what you want, instead of fully surrendering everything to Him. I have been there too. It's when you say something along the lines of, "Oh, this is where God is leading me," but the reality is that you are just slapping His name on your plans.

You can combat this mindset by repenting, submitting your plans to the will of God, and working towards becoming more self-aware. When you are self-aware, you will easily recognize when you are trying to manipulate someone for your gain. Also, it may sound harsh to say that the world doesn't revolve around you, but that's something that I have to tell myself whenever this mindset tries to pop back up in my life.

The Hothead Mindset

This mindset might as well be called "3-2-1, BOOM", because that is how short your fuse is before you end up going off on someone. I don't know about you, but keeping my mouth shut when experiencing injustice, either against myself or a person that I care for, is incredibly difficult. Taking deep breaths and counting to ten is the best way I can calm my nerves and keep myself from saying something that I will end up regretting later. Sometimes I even have to count down from thirty to give myself enough time to diffuse my anger; that is *if* I can remember to stop before opening my mouth. For me, having a full-on outburst of anger typically happens when someone challenges me or rejects my authority. BOOM! There it goes. If you can relate, girl, we have work to do.

You can combat this mindset by exploring who you are really angry at. When God sat me down and asked me who I was really angry at, guess who it turned out to be... *men*. My first hothead moment with a male happened in the third grade on Jersey Day, when my crush made fun of me for rocking a jersey my mom had made because we were too poor to afford a real one. My little heart couldn't handle that; I was LIVID. And then more men trampled on my heart, increasing my anger towards the entire gender.

As you spend time asking yourself who you are really angry at, I would also encourage you to read *Bait of Satan* by John Bevere. And I want to encourage you that while this mindset is difficult to break free from, anger doesn't always have to be bad. Try to turn the things that you are most angry about into righteous anger. Find a cause or a passion that helps others, and use this anger for Kingdom purposes. Fight for others and for God instead of against them.

The Meltdown Mindset

I hate to admit it, but if you ask my mom whether or not I had meltdowns as a child, she would undoubtedly chuckle and say "Yes," with much emphasis on the "s". I wasn't the kind of kid that would throw myself on the floor in a crazy temper tantrum, but I would punch something, throw an item across the room, or shout mean words until I felt like they had cut deep.

While these meltdowns have ceased (praise God), I still experience what I call "Brat Attacks". These are those moments when I find myself whining, "But, God, whyyyyyyy?" They typically occur when I don't get my way, when I don't understand something that God is doing, or when my feelings are hurt.

When God told me to quit my job for the second time, I was actually ready for change, so there was no pushback there. But when it came to the second month of being unemployed, and I had to start wondering where rent was going to come from, I yelled at Him. Meltdowns usually work that way. You keep your composure, reassuring yourself that you're fine again and again, while ignoring the way you actually feel. Every time your emotions rise to the surface, you stuff them back down and bottle them up until… BOOM, the meltdown. I am still trying to break free from this mindset, because I am the type of person who likes to move on quickly from problems. The problem with that, though, is that it is easy for me to forget to feel what I am feeling, when I feel it. So, let's work on this together.

We can combat this mindset by being honest with ourselves and with God. Do not bottle emotions up or try to pretend everything is perfect. God knows what's up. You just need to open up your heart.

The "I Got Me" Mindset

Whew, have I dealt with this one for quite a while. This mindset assures you that you do not need anyone, you cannot trust anyone, and you are "fine by yo'self". While you may be completely awesome, and 40% accurate for believing this, you still need a healthy community. Isolation brings desperation. When you start to isolate yourself, you do dumb things. Take it from me!

During seasons of isolating myself after my feelings had been hurt by other Christian women, I always seemed to end up finding "community" with a man who just wanted some booty. Yeah, I said it. But God designed us to be part of a healthy community. Although Jesus set aside time to be alone, He would always go right back into His relationship with the disciples. If Jesus had community, why shouldn't you? Let that marinate.

You can combat this mindset through prayer. If you are desiring healthy friends, begin praying for them, and watch God place them in your life. If He did it for me, He will for you. I now have friends who love and understand me that I didn't really have in my first two years of being saved. God loves it when we are together in unity—the theme of unity runs through the entire Bible—so believe that He will take care of your need for friendship. Just allow yourself to be open to whomever He brings.

The Money Mindset

Because I grew up in a single parent home, not necessarily having a lot, I have always been drawn to money. And while money is not always a negative thing, it can easily become so, if your heart is in the wrong place. As a former stripper, I had a strong desire for money (to the point of trusting money more than God). When I left that lifestyle and fully gave my life to God, I had to surrender so many things. Certain clothes that were considered to be hoochie or raunchy, perfumes that carried the stench of toxic memories from the club, purses given to me by men, and so on. Materialism and greed are also characteristics connected to this mindset that you might need to pursue freedom from.

As I grew in my relationship with the Lord, the money mindset began to be transformed into a stewardship mindset. I had to learn how to steward what He had given me. I also learned that money itself is NOT the root of all evil, but it's the love of money and the way you prioritize it in your life that can get you into trouble.

You can combat this mindset by asking God to change your heart towards money to be more like His. He will supply you with all that you need to fulfill His purposes for your life; He is faithful. If you align yourself with God, you will not lack anything (John 15).

The Victim Mindset

This mindset likes to bounce back and forth between a "woe is me" attitude and the blame game. It lacks responsibility, never owns up to its faults, and is *always* pointing to other people. If you are struggling with this mindset, remember this: anytime you are eager to point a finger, there are always three pointing right back at you.

My mom told me as a young girl, "Imani, nobody can make you do anything. You are responsible for your own decisions." While I believe that people have influenced some of the decisions that I have made in my life, I was still in the driver seat. It was MY choice to apply for the strip clubs, MY choice to get addicted to drugs, and MY choice to finally follow God. The victim mindset will not get you any level of success in life, nor will it bring you closer to your healing.

How do we combat this mindset? When you feel compelled to blame, call on God's name instead. Ask Him for His wisdom, His insight, and His understanding.

The Misunderstood Mindset

If there is any mindset I can fully relate to, it is this one! If you are a close friend of mine, then you have probably heard me say that I have been misunderstood all of my life. Sometimes the misunderstandings were the result of miscommunication, and other times they were because people had made assumptions about my intentions. While some of these incidents were caused by my actions, the majority of them were due to people seeking to misunderstand me. A friend of mine once advised me to "seek to understand, not to be understood". These wise words have led me to give an immense amount of grace to people.

    What do you want? Do you desire for people to understand your heart? Then go do that for other people! The next time you are in a heated argument or a difficult discussion, I challenge you to really listen and seek to understand. I know it's hard, but trust me. Whatever you pour out will be poured back into you. "Do not be deceived. God cannot be mocked. [You] reap what you sow" (Galatians 6:7)

ALL OF THE MINDSETS LISTED HERE are rooted in fear, control, anger, insecurity, unforgiveness, and rejection. There will be certain circumstances that will try to bring these mindsets back into your head—distorting your view of yourself, God and others—but please run to God when this happens. I know that seeking God isn't often our first response to trials, but if we persist in responding this way, these mindsets will have no choice but to COMPLETELY shake off of us. When we voice our problems to God and praise Him for all that He has already done, we are creating a new mindset.

    There will always be trials, disappointments, and heartbreaks. That is life. But at least when we get to heaven, we will see that it was worth the fight. So, let's fight until we reach eternity. I stand with you, eager to see you conquer these mindsets that try to chain you. Let's pray for each other as we continue to grow and overcome with the grace and strength that we have been given.

Chapter Seven Reflections

1. Which mindsets do you relate to?

2. How have these mindsets hindered your faith, your friendships, and your relationship with God?

3. Pray for freedom in the mindsets that are trying to chain you down. List the mindsets below, and ask God to set you free from each of them.

_____

_____

_____

_____

_____

_____

_____

_____

_____

_____

_____

_____

Chapter 8
THE "GOOD GIRL" IDENTITY CRISIS

When I first accepted Jesus into my heart, I genuinely tried to become a good girl. Taking note of how the other women at church spoke and behaved, I tried to blend in with them by doing everything they did. None of them seemed to have issues with rage, seductive behavior, selfishness or materialism like I did—even my wild laugh felt out of place. So, in order to be like them, I dropped it all. I had even walked away from the friends that I used to dance with, so I could only be around women who loved Jesus. It didn't take long before I became confused. I was so busy trying to be a "good girl", that I had forgotten how to be who God created me to be.

This lasted about two years before I finally found myself again in Jesus. It was spending time with God that ultimately drew me out of the good girl identity crisis. During my times with Him, He revealed pieces of my personality that He had specifically designed for me. He showed me the dreams that He had planted in my heart, and He validated my identity. I no longer needed approval from anyone but Him. So, let me save you the trouble of going down the path that I did. Before you try to chase the good girl identity, stop yourself. You are God's girl, and that is all that matters. I'll say that again. You are God's girl, and that is all that matters.

I really wish that someone had shared this wisdom with me when I first accepted Jesus into my life. While I am sure that God admired my enthusiasm as a new believer, I was so "on fire" for Him that I ended up burning several bridges. I had become critical, judgmental, and impatient—making others feel condemned, unqualified, and misunderstood. Instead of drawing people closer to God, I was pushing them away from Him. I had forgotten where I had come from. I had forgotten my own process and how it had taken me six months to leave the strip club. I had forgotten that I myself fall short of God's glory daily. But it is so easy to forget such truths, when you are caught up in chasing the "good girl" identity and trying to earn the love of God.

See, the problem with the good girl mindset is that it is basically the way the Pharisees behaved back in Jesus' days. While these religious leaders knew the law of Moses by heart, followed all of the prescribed rituals, hosted the religious festivals, and gave the biggest offerings, they lacked true intimacy with God, and they ultimately denied the one person who could save them from themselves (Isaiah 29:13). Jesus made it very clear that He did not like the Pharisees. There were many times in the Bible that He called them out or even cursed them for their bad behavior. But His biggest problem with them was their lack of love towards people that they considered to be sinners—which also happens to the be the root of the problem with the good girl mindset.

For the Son of Man came to seek and save the lost.

- Luke 19:10

Whoever does not love does not know God, because God is love.

- 1 John 4:18

My command is this: love each other as I have loved you.

- John 15:12

If you are busy focusing on convicting or judging people, how can you possibly extend love to them in the moments when they need it most? You can't. And unfortunately, you are missing out on an opportunity to be used by God for His glory.

So, just as the bad girl mindset has to flee, so does the good girl mindset. If you are a former bad girl, you are probably nodding your head and saying, "YAAAS". I'm sure that you are elated to hear that you do not have to trade the bad girl label for the good girl image. Maybe you even questioned whether or not you really wanted to continue this journey, because you didn't want to be called a "good girl". Although you can rest easy in knowing that you do not have to pretend to be anyone else, you still have to let the bad girl go in order to become the woman that God has called you to be.

I understand what it is like to be both the bad girl and the good girl, so I know what I'm talking about here. Truth be told, it was actually more challenging for me to release my good girl ways than the bad girl image. Why? Because I knew that being the bad girl was BAD FOR ME, but it is so easy to be deceived into thinking that the good girl lifestyle is in fact, good. It may appear that way on the outside, but God is not fooled by our actions. He looks much deeper into the intention behind our actions; He looks at our hearts.

To help us sift through both of these mindsets, I would like to share a few verses that highlight what God says about the kind of lifestyle we should pursue:

For by grace you have been saved through faith. And this is not your own doing; it is the gift of God, not a result of works, so that no one may boast.

- Ephesians 2:8-9 (ESV)

Let all that you do be done in love.

- 1 Corinthians 16:14 (ESV)

How is someone with the identity of being God's girl supposed to live? She lives loved and gives love to others, knowing that her Father in heaven sees her, hears her, and wants to do life with her. She isn't running from God, nor is she pretending to have everything figured out. She isn't ashamed to ask for help, but she lives transparently, with an open heart to whatever God intends to do in her life. She believes in who she is and who God says she is: His girl.

Below, I have listed some practical steps to help you live more like God's girl. Personally speaking, the items on this list have helped me in my transformation, and I know they will do the same for you.

- Read the Bible (Philippians 4:8-9)
- Obey God (Deuteronomy 11:1)
- Love God (Mark 12:30-31)
- Love others (Mark 12:30-31)
- Have faith in God (Matthew 21:22)
- Seek & use wisdom (Proverbs 4:6-7)

I want to include one last, yet equally important, aspect that you must remember to do as well: LOVE YOURSELF. Jesus tells us in Scripture to love our neighbors as we love ourselves, but how can we expect to love others well, if we barely love ourselves? We can't.

Maybe you are harboring unforgiveness towards yourself, and it's blocking you from really loving yourself. I get that. I completely understand, girl. There was a time that I was so disgusted with myself for the things I had done, I didn't understand how I could ever love myself. Then I discovered that I could love myself simply because Jesus loves me. Jesus forgave me—He forgave us all—when He died on the cross so that our sins (past, present, and future) could be wiped away. His forgiveness is all that we need in order to forgive ourselves.

And you don't have to hide your story because you feel like you are a hot mess. No, my love. You be the best, most authentic version of yourself that you can be. There are so many people dealing with heartbreak in this world, and they need to hear your story. They desire your transparency and authenticity. One of the most important things that I have learned in my personal journey is that my mistakes are my message. My story is for God's glory. The tests that I have been through—both those that I have passed as well as the ones that I have failed—are part of my testimony. Let them be part of your testimony, too.

Although I admit I have occasionally had some "brat attacks", I no longer claim the bad girl or the good mindset as my own. I am simply God's girl. Former good girl, God's grace is sufficient for everything you need to be in His will (2 Corinthians 12:9). Take ahold of His grace, and let go of the need to be perfect. Former bad girl, I am inviting you to walk in this new identity with us. Let's move on together as God's girls.

Chapter Eight Reflections

1. Do you identify with the "good girl" mindset? How has this hindered your growth with God?

   _____

   _____

   _____

   _____

   _____

2. Do you find it challenging to accept defeat, imperfections and flaws? Why? Where did the idea of perfection begin in your life?

   _____

   _____

   _____

   _____

   _____

3. Loving yourself is sometimes easier said than done. Do you TRULY love yourself?

_____

_____

_____

_____

_____

4. Do you need to forgive yourself for believing any lies about your identity? Do you need to forgive yourself in general? Write a letter to yourself, ending it in a prayer to God.

_____

_____

_____

_____

_____

_____

_____

5. Using the Bible app or Biblegateway.com, search for the word "love," and write the verses that speak to your heart in your journal. Remember to revisit them when you are feeling "less than" or unloved.

Chapter 9

GIVING THEM GRACE, WHEN YOU WANT TO SLAP THEM IN THE FACE!

Cocking my head to the side, I pressed my lips together, trying with all of my might to keep from erupting with rage. Though no one was around to hear me scream, I decided that I would not allow this to make me upset. Still, I felt betrayed, misunderstood, and unheard by someone I had called a friend for a couple of years. I paced around my apartment, trying to collect my thoughts.

No. She. Didn't.

Oh, but she had. Time and time again, I had dealt with friendships that had gone way past their expiration date in my life. My gut had been telling me that this particular friendship was seasonal, but I had become emotionally attached. Although I had initially been reluctant to connect with her, after two years, my walls had finally started to come down. But now, here we were… she was releasing me from her life.

Sure, I could have run to God at that moment, but I wasn't trying to allow any distractions into my schedule. I had things to get done. Instead, I buried my anger and heartbreak and tried to focus on the tasks at hand. Turning some worship music on, I opened my laptop. Moments later, I tossed my laptop to the side, unable to focus. Immediately, I felt God pulling on my heart. I knew He was calling me to run to the throne to talk to Him about how I was feeling.

"Look, God, can we do this later?" I sighed, as I dramatically threw my head back onto the arm of my couch. "I really need to knock out some of these goals before my deadline."

Silence.

The ball was in my court. I knew God wouldn't force me to talk to Him about my feelings, but I also knew what would happen if I didn't address what was happening in my heart. Recalling the way bottling up my feelings had led me to sin in the past, I decided to lay it all on the altar. The song "Build My Life" by Housefires played in the background, shifting the atmosphere in my living room. It didn't take long before all of the hurt that I had been harboring inside of my heart evidenced itself on my face in the form of hot tears.

I remained this way for about fifteen minutes, tears continually falling as I choked back words. The song was on replay, and each time it repeated, my heart received more healing as I reflected on the lyrics and everything God had brought me through. He was there with me, holding my hand as my mascara stained my cheeks. Curling my pillow close to my chest, I heard Him whisper, "I've got you". My anger, my concerns, my tears, they all mattered to Him.

This particular incident played out very different than it would have before Jesus became a part of my life. So, yes, you read the title of this chapter correctly. While your initial reaction might not be to slap someone in the face when they have wronged you, that has not been the case for me.

When you don't have a relationship with someone, it can be fairly easy to brush off their rude remarks, judgments, or even slander. But getting hurt by people that you love... that is an entirely different level of trust that can be robbed from you. If you aren't careful, they can wound you so deeply that it causes you to backtrack in your spiritual progression. But if you respond as Jesus would, these painful situations can actually advance your spiritual growth. Responding like Jesus would isn't always easy, and He warned us that it wouldn't be, but it is possible.

If you love those who love you, what credit is that to you? Even sinners love those who love them. And if you do good to those who are good to you, what credit is that to you? Even sinners do that. And if you lend to those from whom you expect repayment, what credit is that to you? Even sinners lend to sinners, expecting to be repaid in full. But love your enemies, do good to them, and lend to them without expecting to get anything back. Then your reward will be great, and you will be children of the Most High, because he is kind to the ungrateful and wicked. Be merciful, just as your Father is merciful.

- Luke 6:32-36

Bless those who persecute you; bless and do not curse. Rejoice with those who rejoice, and weep with those who weep. Be of the same mind toward one another; do not be haughty in mind, but associate with the lowly Do not be wise in your own estimation. Never pay back evil for evil to anyone Respect what is right in the sight of all men. If possible, so far as it depends on you, be at peace with all men. Never take your own revenge, beloved, but leave room for the wrath of God, for it is written, "VENGEANCE IS MINE, I WILL REPAY," says the Lord. "BUT IF YOUR ENEMY IS HUNGRY, FEED HIM, AND IF HE IS THIRSTY, GIVE HIM A DRINK; FOR IN SO DOING YOU WILL HEAP BURNING COALS ON HIS HEAD." Do not be overcome by evil, but overcome evil with good.

- Romans 12:14-21

Why is it that the people that we love hurt us the most? And why is it that Christians—people who are supposed to KNOW JESUS—can hurt us so deeply, when they should know better?

Why do the people that you have forgiven numerous times repeatedly make the same mistakes?

And why is it so hard to love those who persecute you?

What if I told you that the hardest things that we have to experience on this Earth have a heavenly reward attached to them? Loving those who cause us pain, seeking forgiveness, and asking Jesus to help you see things the way that He does, brings you a reward and a victory.

Blessed are the pure in heart, for they shall see God. Blessed are the peacemakers, for they shall be called sons of God. Blessed are those who have been persecuted for the sake of righteousness, for theirs is the kingdom of heaven. Blessed are you when people insult you and persecute you, and falsely say all kinds of evil against you because of Me. Rejoice and be glad, for your reward in heaven is great; for in the same way they persecuted the prophets who were before you.

Matthew 5:8-12

Consider it all joy, my brethren, when you encounter various trials, knowing that the testing of your faith produces endurance. And let endurance have its perfect result, so that you may be perfect and complete, lacking in nothing. But if any of you lacks wisdom, let him ask of God, who gives to all generously and without reproach, and it will be given to him.

- James 1:2-5

I can't say that this is a simple step-by-step method. I wish. Girl, do I wish! But I can tell you that if we DON'T go to God with our grief and pain, our progress will be paused, or we may lose our progress altogether. Do you remember the bad girl and good girl mindsets we previously discussed? If we aren't intentional with running to the throne, they will return. Do not harbor your hurt in your heart. Do not return to your Bad Girl Blues. Just let it out.

Next, comes the grace part. We have previously discussed that in order to be God's girl, love has to be at the core of all we do. God is love, and if He lives inside of us, His love should be evident to everyone around us. Well, grace depends solely on whether or not we truly understand how to love others, because grace basically says that we are supposed to extend that love to the ones in our lives that we consider loveless; the ones who have hurt us and seem undeserving of our love. To give someone grace is basically to respond to their hurtful actions with gentleness, kindness, and love.

Giving people grace when you want to slap them in the face is not easy. At all. It's almost like having to work out at the gym after months of sitting on your couch watching television. Even though the thought of going back to the gym is dreadful, you go because you know it's good for you. And then, of course, after your workout, you feel a sense of pride in yourself for having gone through with it (not to mention the rush of endorphins that boost your mood). However, the next day, you are sore. But sore muscles mean that strength is building, and if you stay consistent with your workout routine, you will see incredible results.

Giving grace is hard, and it hurts, but because Jesus offers us grace when we least deserve it, we have to extend it to others as well. When you do this, you prove to the enemy that you are not a slave to your flesh or your emotions; you show God that you are committed to working out your grace muscles; and you give yourself the opportunity to heal and create healthy boundaries for yourself.

Although grace does forgive and extend love even in tough situations, it is important to note that being a gracious person does not mean that you have to resign yourself to being someone's door mat. Sometimes you have to give grace from a distance. Giving someone grace doesn't mean that you have to remain in their face or be buddy, buddy with them. In some cases, you need to identify how much space you need and for how long. There are some people who have hurt me, but they're still in my life. We may not talk as frequently as we used to, but I still love them and have forgiven them. And there are others who have been completely cut out of my life, because I know what I can handle. I still love them, and I have offered grace, but now I keep them several spaces from me.

Involve Jesus and seek His wisdom on the decision that needs to be made, and then answer yourself honestly. And if you are meant to be connected with that person, God will bring him or her back around in the right time. But in the meantime, protect your space, your mind, and your heart, while extending the same grace that you have been given from God.

If it is a friend that has betrayed you, give her grace.

If it is your mom or dad that has neglected you, give them grace.

If it is the church community that hurt you, give them grace.

If it is a coworker whom you choose to confide in and she broke your trust, give her grace.

Whatever the case may be, everyone deserves grace, because we all sin and fall short of God's glory (Romans 3:23). We are all well aware of the mistakes that we have made in life, and we are also aware that we are truly undeserving of God's love and grace. So, if GOD HIMSELF can give us grace for all of the jacked up mistakes we have made, we need to learn how to offer it to people who have wronged us. Do you understand that we were once condemned to HELL because of the fall in the garden of Eden? Hell, y'all—hot, stinky, dirty, dusty, crusty, scary hell. But God offered Jesus to die for our sins, and His grace is offered to us every time we fall short of His expectations for us.

Now, I have to be honest with you (at this point in the book, you should expect no less from me). Grace is not usually the first option I choose when I get hurt by someone, and I'm sure you could probably say the same. Personally, as a woman who is passionate about seeking justice, I have to wrestle with the idea of not always being able to "check" someone when I feel they are out of line. God has helped me grow in this area, and He is teaching me that I can still confront people when they are doing something wrong, but only when I am in a heart posture of grace with the individual. If I lack grace, then I lack the seasoning of love on my words, and everything I say will be like rubbing salt on an open wound. And no one wants that.

So, give the people in your life the grace they need to make mistakes, and then give yourself some space to heal. And if you are being intentional with your healing and staying close to God, in due time, you will become stronger, more compassionate, and in a headspace where you can truly live like God's girl.

Chapter Nine Reflections

1. How do you typically respond when someone breaks your trust?

   _____

   _____

   _____

   _____

   _____

2. When you get hurt, do you find yourself running to the throne or the phone?

   _____

   _____

   _____

   _____

   _____

   _____

   _____

3. Take a moment to pray and sit with the Holy Spirit. Who do you need to forgive today?

　

4. Do you find it difficult to give others grace? Reflect on the circumstances, mistakes, and decisions you have made in your life that have hurt Jesus. How has His grace helped you overcome these decisions?

Chapter 10
TRUSTING THEM

"Aye, you see where my shirt went?" S searched through my messy room, getting no help from me. I lay on the bed physically satisfied, but emotionally distant from both him and myself—a feeling I was all too familiar with.

"Nope. I actually don't think you came over wearing one. You had a jacket though. I think it's downstairs." I slowly rose from the bed to escort him down my townhome stairs to the hall closet.

"Well, you can have the rest of the weed, if you want. I need to stop by my plug to get more anyway." He handed me the sack from his jacket pocket.

That would help me feel a little better, but what I really wanted was to lock him inside my home and ask him a million questions about why he wouldn't love me, what was wrong with me, and any other question my crazy mind could possibly come up with. Instead, I just smiled and said, "Thanks, S. I'll let you know how I feel after work this week. I may want you to come over."

He smirked and hugged me as he made his way out the door. It was 4 a.m., and I had just gotten home from the club. I would often invite S over after work, whether it had been a rough night or a good money-making night. Although he wasn't my boyfriend (he basically cringed at the mention of the word), he was pretty cool to hang out with, and he was never disrespectful or rude to me. When we would hang, we would smoke and talk about business, books, music, and other topics of that nature, but it always ended the same way—with him walking out of the door, never giving me what my heart desperately wanted.

"SO, WHEN DO YOU THINK you'll settle down, Imani?" my friend asked. "I mean, I get that you stopped dating females and chose not to be a player anymore… and, yeah, you narrowed it down to one guy that you're sleeping with right now, but don't you want a boyfriend?"

I knew she meant well, but the timing of her question was terrible. She and everyone else in our circle had boyfriends; everyone except me. This had become the norm for me, but as I was running out of decent prospects, my friends were beginning to get worried for me. All of the men I was interested in were incredibly attractive, but being well aware of this fact, they knew how to use their looks to their advantage. Yup, they were players. But I was also well aware of their games, so I was careful to protect my heart so that I never allowed myself to actually catch any feelings for them. I kept everything on the surface… well, everything except sex. I couldn't allow myself to trust anyone, because it always produced the same result: heartbreak.

Not in the mood to talk about my dating life, I grabbed my weed, lit a bowl, and took a deep inhale before answering her. "You know what, girl? I'm done having sex, period. I'm cutting off both men and women, and that includes S. I'm done feeling like an object to men at the club, and then coming home and not getting the love I need from the men in my personal life. I honestly don't want a real relationship right now, but I know that having sex isn't helping my situation either."

I continued making grand declarations about my sex life, as my friend listened, chiming in every once in a while with a couple of "Yeah, girls" and "Mhmms".

As soon as we got off the phone, I texted S and shared my new plan for celibacy. He responded, "LOL! Okay, coo".

No, it wasn't "coo", and that was exactly why I hadn't given him my heart in the first place. And man, was I happy that I hadn't.

ABOUT A YEAR BEFORE I began writing this book, I asked God to restore my ability to trust men. Over the years, my heart had hardened towards men, and I lacked even basic compassion for them. In my opinion, they were all either egotistical or highly insecure—traits which I found to be incredibly annoying. I knew that I had become very critical of men, but I also knew that these same men were God's princes, and He loved them just as much as He loved me. Something in me had to change.

Ultimately, my prayer for God to change my feelings towards men led me directly into having to deal with rejection from a man I really liked. Though it would seem that what happened is the exact opposite of what I had asked God to do, it actually brought me face-to-face with past issues of rejection I had bottled up for years. Through this situation, God opened my eyes. He did so in many ways, but one of the main ways He opened my eyes was by giving me a dream that illustrated the journey of a man from infanthood to manhood.

    Imagine a young boy, around the age of seven, who has grown up in a household with a physically and emotionally absent father. There is an unspoken pressure on the boy to become the man of the house and be strong for his mother and his siblings—though he has never been shown what a real man actually is supposed to look like. Fast forward years later to when he has become a teenager. His face has hardened, as the stress of life weighs heavily on his young heart. He has no place of safety; no one that he can confide in. His mom is trying to be the strongest she can for his family, so not wanting to add any additional stress on her shoulders, he looks for comfort elsewhere. It doesn't take long for him to find it in gangs, women, drugs, and partying—anything that validates his manhood.

    Then God showed me the way the teenage boy had been influenced by his surroundings instead of the pure love his heart had been created to experience. Perhaps this teenage boy finds what he identifies as love when he becomes attracted to a woman who captures his attention. She is safe. She is his. But not for long. Unbeknownst to him, she has her own insecurities and hurt that she's dealing with, which eventually lead her to move on to another guy. Taking up the pieces of his broken heart, the young man decides to pursue the identity of the "bad boy", since that seems to be what girls like.

Please understand that I am NOT trying to offer excuses for men to be liars or disrespectful. Not at all. I am just sharing what God showed me. He used a scenario that resembles my personal story in order to help me empathize with men and develop compassion towards them. I believe that if you truly desire to soften your heart towards men, then God will show you exactly what you need to see as well. This dream was the beginning of my heart being softened for His sons (my brothers), and one day my husband.

God also walked me down memory lane of my personal life, exposing one of the biggest reasons I had decided to date women. As you may have guessed, it was mainly due to the various types of betrayal I had experienced by the men in my life—starting with my father. Not feeling protected by him in childhood greatly contributed to my belief that there wasn't any man that desired to protect me. With my heart for men depleting, but the longing to be loved still very real, I went looking for love in the arms of a woman. While this is not always the case for women that proclaim themselves to be lesbians, it was for me—among other negative experiences with men, like being taken advantage of sexually and getting drugged, raped, and rejected. But little did I realize that women would hurt me just as much as men, and oftentimes even more.

God also showed me that I had been trying to fill a void in my heart, and as a result, I had allowed my heart to be repeatedly stepped on. Inevitably, my heart became calloused and hard. God really wanted to press in on this prayer of mine, so He led me to write down all of the memories that I had with men. I know, you probably just got upset for me, but I promise it wasn't a heartbreaking experience, because I had already gone through it before with God. No, this time the assignment was to show me unhealthy patterns in my life that had led to my mistrust of men. This process also allowed me to truly forgive a few men from a deep place within my heart instead of through empty words. While it was painful, it was rewarding in the end, because it brought me to a new understanding of how to trust men that I am able to share with you.

If you have issues with trusting men, I want you to write out your memories with the men in your life like I did. But first, I need you to be mentally prepared. If you have a hot mess past like myself, you may begin to feel shameful or dirty. Girl, if it makes you feel any better, when I was writing my list, I struggled with remembering some of the guys' names! If you have been cheated on or lied to like myself, you may feel bitterness arise. I want you to feel these emotions, because more than likely, they're resurfacing because you suppressed them instead of handling them in a healthy way. Even as all of these emotions arise, I want you to remember a few important truths. You may have made mistakes, but you are not a mistake. You have been forgiven and redeemed, and God has marked you as His princess.

    Trusting men has been challenge for me all my life. As you know, my track record with men hasn't been the best or the holiest. Maybe you can relate. As I wrote out my memories with men, I went way, way, way back to elementary school. Remember the "Jersey Day" fiasco I mentioned earlier? That is where my journey of not trusting men began. It was followed with neglect from my dad, rape at the age of twelve, rejection from my half-brother who denied being related to me the first (and only) day that he met me, and then more men playing mind games with me only to get "you know what" from me. This exercise with God led me to the names of numerous men and women, but more importantly, it also led me to discover the person that I am today: a woman pursuing healing for herself with her Savior, unashamed of her past and focused on bringing others to their healing as well.

God wants to set us free to be able to love and trust the men in our lives, but we have to actively pursue this freedom and prepare our hearts to trust again. Otherwise...

How do you plan to get married, if you can't trust men?

How do you anticipate having a healthy marriage, if you can't trust your husband?

How do you expect to receive correction and love from your pastor, if you can't believe the words that come out of a man's mouth?

How do you plan to grow a relationship with God as your Father, if you don't trust Him as such?

I can promise you this: obtaining this freedom will be difficult, if you choose to roll your eyes and hide behind the walls you created from past trust issues and pain. So, what does the pursuit of trusting men entail? It begins with trusting God.

I want you to do something with me. Close your eyes, take a deep breath, and ask yourself if you really trust God. Ask God to reveal moments where you have had to lean on Him instead of yourself. Now, sit still and wait for Him to show those moments to you. If you don't recall anything, ask God if you actually trust Him. Write down what He says. It is usually a "yes" or "no" answer, so if God says "No", ask Him to reveal the area of your life that you do not trust Him in. Stop here and take some time to follow these steps, then meet me back here when you are done.

I know that I can trust God to provide for my finances and to protect me. I even trust God enough to take tremendous leaps of faith when He asks me to. But I haven't always fully trusted Him to write my love story. I always have something to interject about His plans for my future husband. But to fully trust God means that you believe with all of your heart that He is faithful and not a liar. I know that God will bring me a MAN OF GOD who will know exactly how to love me; a man I can call my best friend. But how do I surrender my trust issues to Him so that I can fully trust that He will do it?

    I am still figuring this one out, but I want to say once again that it begins with keeping it real with God. Let Him know your fears, concerns, and reservations for whatever it is that you are finding it difficult to trust Him in. And after doing this, I believe finding scriptures to combat those fears is important. You can't just identify a lie without bringing truth to it. You have to dig into your Bible or google verses on trust and then write them down in your journal. These will become your emergency Bible verses that will help you during tough times. My personal favorite is Proverbs 3:5-6:

> *Trust in the Lord with all your heart and lean not on your own understanding; in all your ways submit to him, and he will make your paths straight.*

At this point, you have told God why you feel it's hard to trust Him, and you have prepared your heart with scripture. Now, you need to pray. In fact, I want to pray with you.

Lord, my sweet and sovereign Father—free of worry and distress, and full of love for me. I want to thank you, God, for being faithful, for being present, and for choosing to love me despite my trust issues with you. I thank you for always showing up and taking care of me, even when I forget to praise you. Thank you, Abba. You are a loving and beautiful God.

Lord, please transform my heart and perspective. Help me to trust you, and please heal any piece of me that is causing me to distrust you. Help me to see things the way that you do. Give me your understanding and your peace to pursue trusting you. I ask that you draw me closer to you, daily. I ask that you show me your ever-abiding presence in the midst of my life. I thank you for sending the Holy Spirit as my helper, and for offering your peace. I love you, Lord. In Jesus' name, amen.

I am praying this with you, and I know that if we draw near to Him, He will bring us closer to Himself. And within that closeness, we will learn how to trust again.

Chapter Ten Reflections

1. Have you found it hard to trust men? When did this mistrust begin in your life?

2. God is referred to as our Father. Do you find it difficult to trust God because He is a male?

3. Ask God to show you what you need to know to help you understand why men behave the way that they do. Write down the experience you have and what you have learned during this process.

_____

_____

_____

_____

_____

_____

_____

_____

_____

_____

_____

_____

_____

Chapter 11
THE DANGERS OF DETACHMENT

Ugh. See, this is why you shouldn't give a damn about anyone, Imani. People can't act right, and they always end up breaking your heart. This is why you don't get attached to people. If you would've stayed detached, you wouldn't have had to go through this process right now. But nope, you ended up letting yourself love her, and look at you now, girl—a hot mess with a whole journey of healing ahead of you.

I lay on my bed, feeling completely numb. I didn't have the words to describe what I was feeling, but I knew that I wasn't trying to feel whatever it was. I grabbed my phone to re-read the text from my friend.

"How do you feel right now?"

The hell if I knew.

Being emotionally detached was a defense mechanism that I had acquired at a young age. I figured if I was detached from someone, then there would be a smaller chance for me to get heartbroken when they inevitably hurt me. It made sense in my mind, and it seemed like a smart way of controlling who had access to my feelings. This defense mechanism was supposed to help me protect myself, but all it ended up doing was hurting me in the end.

Detachment started for me around the age of ten, when my dad brought another family into our lives, causing me to feel rejected and unworthy. It was in that moment that I had determined that I would never allow anyone to make me feel that way again. The pain of that moment had pierced my heart so thoroughly that I decided that nobody could ever get that close to me, unless I allowed them to. As I got older, the detachment grew stronger every time a person walked out of my life or a family member gossiped about me. In my struggle to find my identity, I always ran back to the detachment mechanism, until it eventually became my strength.

So how was I feeling?

Maybe I needed to cry. I closed my eyes, trying to force the tears to fall, but nothing happened. Man, I had become such a beast at being detached that I couldn't even understand my heart and emotions, let alone control them. Then it clicked. I had become detached from myself.

If I had been attached to myself, I never would have decided to strip. Instead, I would have known how valuable and precious I was as a woman.

If I had been attached to myself, I never would have run to women to fill my emotional needs. Instead, I would have known that it was hatred towards men that was leading me to women, not because they could love me any better than a man could.

If I was attached to myself, I never would have allowed drugs to enter my body. Instead, I would have saved so much time, money, and brain cells, knowing that the high was fleeting and only temporarily filling a void.

If I was attached to myself, I never would have thrown my hands at another woman. Instead, I would have kept it cute and mute, knowing that her words were caused by her own insecurities.

If I was attached to myself, I never would have gone to jail due to reckless behavior. Instead, I would have spent my time doing activities that added value to my life.

Upon receiving this realization, release finally came. As the tears ran down my cheeks, I realized how much hurt *I* had brought upon myself. It wasn't anyone else's fault. Yeah, the behavior of some people didn't help some of the situations I had faced in life, but it was because of my own detachment from myself that I had experienced a lot of things that God had never intended for me to experience. The realizations continued to flood my mind…

If I were attached to myself, I would have recognized that I needed God in the very depth of my soul. And if I were attached to God, I would be writing a very different book right now with a completely different story.

As I wiped away tears, I had to catch myself from falling into the pit of self-hatred. Re-establishing the attachment with myself meant that I needed to show myself love, and from that point on, I was going to do so.

Detachment tells us that nobody can love us, and that keeping yourself from making connections with others is the "strong" way of living. You go through life barely trusting anyone, and you end up living isolated, which can lead you into detachment depression. I promise you, you do not want to proceed with living this way. Take it from someone who has lived detached for several years of her life. This lightbulb moment didn't happen for me until the fourth year of my salvation. If you are reading this now, make it your personal prayer and mission to live loved and to let go of detachment mechanisms.

Now, just because we decide to let go of the detachment mechanisms doesn't mean we just go around freely giving out trust to everyone. No, girl, you will end up hating people if you do that. Instead, we are going to replace detachment with discernment. Discernment is the ability to see with your spiritual eyes into someone else's heart and intentions. You know when you first meet someone, and you get a sense that something is "off" about them spiritually? That, my friend, is discernment. It is a gift that is given from Yahweh Himself to help us live a more healthy and holy lifestyle. Without discernment, we make dumb choices based off of our often shaded perspective, leading us into regret, heartbreak, and hatred.

    Use discernment and prayer to guide you in making decisions that were once guided by detachment. For example, if you have a new friendship, and you're reluctant to get close to the person, take a moment to pause and pray. Ask yourself and God if the detachment mechanism is telling you that she isn't worthy of your trust or if you are discerning something deeper. This is probably going to be difficult to determine at first, but if you have a track record of pushing away people due to detachment, more than likely, the old habit is resurfacing in this new friendship. I suggest that you give the person opportunities to connect with you, and during that time, observe her character, pray about the purpose of this new friendship, and then ask God how to move forward. You don't know unless you try, girl.

    Now, on the other hand, let's say that your discernment is telling you that this friendship is done. In cases like these, you have to make the decision to detach from the person, but in a healthy way. After all that talk about detachment being a bad thing, detaching yourself from someone in a healthy manner probably sounds very impossible. How do we even do such a thing? If we aren't careful, we can end up back at square one in the detached mechanism, but I have experienced that there are healthy ways to detach yourself from someone. It requires cleansing your heart from anything negative or toxic that you may feel towards that person. Once you do this, you will want to ask God to give you HIS perspective on how He views the person. Girl, I promise this works. You will have to do it consistently, and you may even need to unfollow them from social media, delete their number, get mad for a moment, or cry, but it will work.

If you have lived with the detachment mechanism all of your life, then you have probably also been detached from yourself. I need to warn you that if you aren't focused on releasing the negative detachment mindset, you will never be able to truly love yourself, neither will you be able to experience the fullness of God, because we can only fully know God when we attach ourselves to Him (see Jeremiah 33:3 and John 15).

When you decide to attach yourself to God, you begin the journey of getting to know your Creator. It is a beautiful journey, and you will never want to look back. On this journey, you identify the characteristics of God and the deeper details of His personality, His mission, and how much He loves you. You learn about Him as Abba Father, Elohim the Creator, and Yahweh-Rapha your Healer, as He continues to take you from glory to glory in His presence.

In this space of being attached to the One who designed your innermost being, you will finally be able to attach with yourself, and you cannot even begin to imagine how exciting being in this space with God can be. So, make the decision today to choose discernment over detachment and to attach your heart to God, and ultimately to yourself.

Chapter Eleven Reflections

1. Do you have a hard time being vulnerable with people? Why is that?

   _____

   _____

   _____

   _____

   _____

2. What have your recent experiences in friendships been like? Would you say that you are vulnerable with your friends and that you trust them?

   _____

   _____

   _____

   _____

   _____

3. Prayerfully reflect on your past. Do you see how detachment with others has caused you to be detached from yourself?

4. Make a commitment to God and yourself to always be attached to Him. Write this promise in your journal.

Chapter 12
PLAYING TUG-OF-WAR WITH GOD

God knows I would much rather be writing the novel I was working on than the book you are currently reading. Don't get me wrong, I am blessed to have a story that many women can relate to, but writing a nonfiction book is not ideal for me. I was actually halfway through writing one of my favorite fictional books, fully infatuated with the characters and the plot, when God interrupted my flow. He directed me to pause on my novel and to begin praying about this book.

Those prayers led me to write a manuscript, only to toss it out three times. You can imagine how much that motivated me to write this fourth one... it didn't. But it did lead to sharing my testimony publicly on my YouTube channel. Writing this book also connected me to the Writers Retreat, giving me the opportunity to meet other women who were writing their first books, and it allowed me to fulfill a lifelong dream of going to

Santorini, Greece. While all of this is incredible, I still would much rather be writing my novel right now.

This may sound like a big rant or maybe even a "rebellion against God" to some of you, and I'm sorry if it sounds that way, but let's be honest. How many of us have tried to play tug-of-war with God over something that He told us to release? Maybe you have an ex that you KNOW you need to block, but nope, you still have access to him and he still has access to you. Perhaps you know you need to leave your current church home, because God has called you to leave it. Or maybe you have been told to quit your job, but because that doesn't make any logical sense to you, you don't want to do it. Whatever your situation may be, we have all experienced what it's like to have a tug-of-war with God.

Clearly, this book was written. You are holding proof of my obedience to God in your hands right now. I surrendered my novel to God, because I knew that writing this one first was much more important. I mean, Yahweh said so Himself. But that doesn't mean I didn't procrastinate when it came to getting this God-given task done, nor does it mean the process of writing this book was always a cheerful one for me. No, I still had moments where I wanted to run to my novel and pick up where I had left off. There were even moments when I just wanted to pause and resume writing this book years later, since that seemed to be the prevalent opinion from other people.

Procrastination is rooted in fear, and I procrastinated and often ran from writing this book because I was afraid of what was to follow. Would people judge me? Would I even succeed? And what exactly did I expect to happen after publishing this book? Would people like what I had to say? What would people at my job say? I had a ton of thoughts and fears trying to consume my mind.

You're more than likely playing tug-of-war with God for similar reasons. Maybe you're procrastinating on something because you're afraid that you will fail or that you're not hearing God correctly. Maybe you're procrastinating because you don't believe that God will truly provide for ALL of your needs. Or maybe you are scared because you're holding onto a person or a dream that you know God wants you to release. Releasing my ex-girlfriend was the longest tug-of-war I had with God.

Yes.

You read that correctly.

Of all the things that I have mentioned thus far, releasing her was one of the hardest things that I had to surrender. I had developed a strong emotional attachment to her, so letting her go was easier said than done. And trusting that God would help me understand why this was difficult for me was a foreign concept. Even after growing in my relationship with God, I believed that if I felt the way I did towards her, I would be condemned to hell and that God would hate me. So, I kept this struggle to myself.

We privately dated for two years, and then once I got saved, we tried to remain friends for three years. As a Christian woman, I have no place but to love everyone, no matter what their sexual preference or identity may be. The same applies to you, too. That being said, I want to ensure that you understand that I did not cut her out of my life because of her sexuality. I stress this point because there are so many people you might be called to love who live differently than you, but your job as a Christian is to love them and reflect the love of Jesus. Period.

This particular woman was released from my life because she was an ex, and ANY EX needs a next. My ex boyfriends had all been quickly dismissed from my life, therefore she needed to be dismissed as well. The man that I end up marrying should not need to worry about ANY exes calling me, regardless of their sex, and I know FOR SURE I would not tolerate it myself. Aside from that, God had made it very clear that there was a soul tie between the two of us. So, yes, she had to go.

    The reason why I pulled so hard against God on this was because I really wanted her to be part of my life. Yes, she was an ex, but she was also a friend. While I had no intention of running back into that lifestyle once I had left, Satan is slick, and the flesh is weak. God also knows both of His daughters, and He knew that our relationship would have hindered my healing as wells as hers. God was also extremely jealous that she had taken up so much residency in my heart. Instead of spending time daydreaming or chatting it up with God, I would invite her into these moments. Anyone or anything that gets more of your time than God is an idol, and it will eventually need to go.

    So why was I holding so tightly onto the rope?

    I had no idea. I needed to ask God what was going on within my heart. I needed to slow down and have a conversation with Him about the condition of my heart. I needed to accept His invitation to connect with Him.

> *Search me, God, and know my heart; test me and know my anxious thoughts. See if there is any offensive way in me and lead me in the way everlasting.*
>
>   - Psalms 139:23-24

I had spent too much time ignoring the elephant in the room, and it was time for me to face it head on. This time I wasn't just passively complying with God's desires for me, but I was completely abandoning myself to His will. Please understand that passive compliance is not real obedience. Just because you choose to obey God because of your fear of missing out, going to hell, or whatever, it does not mean that you will not have to deal with the same internal struggle again at some point in the future. We need to get to the place where we can have these real and raw conversations with God. If you are truly asking for help from a heart posture of desiring healing, God will answer your questions. My questions sounded like: Why did I still have feelings for her? Why was I even attracted to women in the first place? Why does she have to leave my life? Why is it so hard to let her go?

I cried my heart out to God that night and eventually opened up to three mature friends who embraced me during that difficult time. They didn't judge me or beat me over the head with scripture that I already knew. They didn't sound shocked or confused, making me feel awkward. They just loved me, and they still love me.

God lovingly walked me back to where same sex attraction had been introduced to me as a young girl. He showed me how my childlike curiosity from daycare and my eventual introduction to pornography was a part of the pull towards women. He showed me how the trust issues I had developed with men pulled me towards women. God took His time walking me through every question that I had, because that is what a loving Father does.

God was giving me a deeper understanding about myself and who He is, and I was an active participant in this experience. If I had decided to only passively comply, I would have missed out on this opportunity, and I would have ended up in the same cycle. If I would have chosen to handle this on my own, I would have missed out on getting to know the compassionate women God placed in my life to walk with me through that moment. I would have been too scared to share the struggles that I was dealing with, and as a result, I would have run from them. But God doesn't call us to live in fear. He wants us to run to Him with questions, seeking His knowledge and His healing hands.

> *There is no fear in love. But perfect love drives out fear, because fear has to do with punishment. The one who fears is not made perfect in love.*
>
> - 1 John 4:18

I share all of this with you because I want you to know that I understand what it is like to have a tug-of-war with God. Whether you are being called to let a same sex relationship go, or it's your ex-boyfriend that needs to go, God is telling you that you have to trust that He will fill that void in your heart. God wants to be my friend that I can daydream with, review my goals with, and discuss my ideas with. He also wants to bring me a super fine, spiritually and physically fit man to live the rest of my life with. But if I am not trusting God, and I'm holding onto a friendship that He has commanded me to let go, then I am telling God that I don't need Him or His plans.

Surrender whatever (or whoever) God is telling you to release. If it isn't an intimate relationship, but a friendship, girl I have been there too. I have lost friends that I used to hang out with when I wasn't saved, as well as Christian friends. I have released friends that I had imagined spending vacations and play dates with. And just so we're clear, God isn't telling you to release them because He is in Heaven being bossy or wanting to dominate your life. Please do not think that is why, because we can easily slip into believing that lie. But it is truly because God knows things that we don't know, and He is protecting us from things that will hurt us if we aren't careful.

Now that you have identified why you are playing tug-of-war with God, ask God to show you when the tug-of-war began in your life. How is this blocking you from experiencing the fullness of God? Do you *truly* believe that God will take care of all of your needs? If you answered no, please take some time to write out why you are struggling with this belief. Oftentimes, it is because of rejection or abandonment that we faced from our earthly father that causes a lack of trust with God. Search your heart with God and write down what He reveals. Once you know the root and the lie that is causing you to cling onto control instead of surrendering, release it, and embrace the following truths listed below:

- Release it with the knowledge that your Father loves you (John 3:16).
- Release it, knowing that God has a plan for you (Jeremiah 29:11).
- Release it, knowing that you CANNOT FAIL when you are with God (Psalms 46:5)
- Release it, knowing that God will direct your steps (Proverbs 3:5-6).
- Release it, knowing that if you abide in Jesus, everything you ask for will be done (John 15).

I know how challenging this can be, and I don't expect you to just breeze through this chapter and then *voila*, you're the most surrendered to God sister out in these streets. No. I know it doesn't work that way with deep matters of the heart. God also knows this truth, and He offers us grace every time we try to take matters into our own hands, but I just want you to remember that while He does give grace, He is a whole lot smarter than us. If we listen to Him in the first place, we can save ourselves a whole lot of heartache. He is on our side, and He is the ONLY one you need on your side. When you feel scared, lonely, or even just bored, don't run back to what you have released.

You will be tested. I was tested and failed so many times. But you have to stand strong in the promises of God, as you surround yourself with women of God who will love you through the struggle, yet check your whole life up if they need to. Get around women who want to see you win, women who will fight with you and for you. And if you don't have that right now, girl, pray for it. In the meantime, find a good church home, watch sermons online as you get ready for work, and just feed your spirit with the Word of God. If you are not full on the Word, you will be full on something else, and we both know that something else isn't going to satisfy you. Anything but Jesus will leave a void in your heart. Let's pray together.

Thank You, Abba, for loving me. Thank you for being so patient with me, even when I am undeserving and just completely tripping out on you. Thank you for pursuing me relentlessly because of your love for me. Thank you for actually loving me during all phases of my life. Lord, I ask that you help me adore the things that you adore. Help me desire your will and your ways. Help me to enjoy what you delight in. I want to surrender and release all that you have called me to release (list it out here):

_____

_____

_____

_____.

I ask that you would help me stay free from these things. God, I thank you for providing for all of my needs, and for filling any voids in my heart. You understand me, and you know me. Continue to make me more like you. In Jesus' name, amen.

Chapter Twelve Reflections

1. This is probably a tough chapter to work through, but it is necessary for our growth. What have you been holding onto that God is asking you to release?

   _____

   _____

   _____

   _____

   _____

2. Why do you think you struggle with releasing this to God?

   _____

   _____

   _____

   _____

   _____

3. Have you questioned whether or not God has your back? Why is this a struggle for you?

_____

_____

_____

_____

_____

_____

_____

_____

_____

_____

_____

4. Make a decision to trust in God, and meditate on Proverbs 3:5-6.

Chapter 13
WAY MAKER, MIRACLE WORKER, PROMISE KEEPER

If you have been in church recently, you probably are familiar with the title of this chapter. If you are anything like me, you probably even started singing the song. If you haven't heard it, girl, then get on it! Look up "Way Maker" by Sinach before you read this chapter, and just play the song. I won't go anywhere. Go experience God in worship, because this song has so much power and revelation about who God is. I love this song because I have found it to be so true. God is a way maker, a miracle worker, and a promise keeper. He has shown this to be true so many times in my life, that I know that He will never forsake you or me.

When you decide to follow Him, and you open up your heart to Him, then you will begin to encounter Him. Encountering Jesus means encountering miracles, promises fulfilled, and opportunities that you never believed you were even "qualified" to receive. Encountering Jesus means breakthrough, healing, freedom, and fun! Yes, fun is included.

I am actually about to get off topic here, but it is crazy how I once thought that Christians lived boring lives. The problem with this thought is that it actually is true for some Christians. Some people are living scared, afraid to make faith moves, scared to really live a life that models Jesus', because they don't want any backlash from Satan or his crazy kids. Some Christians are living a dull and boring life because they are "too holy" or "too sanctified", living completely away from those who do not know Jesus, completely missing what real evangelism entails. And some are just legit unaware of who God is and who He created them to be. Therefore, they stay stuck working boring jobs they hate, never really tapping into their true purpose.

But this does NOT mean that Jesus doesn't want us to have fun. I know plenty of believers who are experiencing a real life encounter with Jesus and living their best life. They are the people who know God and know themselves in Him, which allows them to have healthy relationships with others. They have made some moves that require some level of trust in God, they have surrendered to God even when it hurts, and they have testimonies for days to glorify God for all that He has done in their lives. These people are producing fruit in their marriage, ministry, business, joy, and in their influence with people. And if your life is producing fruit, it means that you are having a fun life with Jesus.

God is a way maker, a miracle worker, and a promise keeper. The best way to live out this revelation of who God is, is to recall the amazing things that He has done in your life. If you are a new Christian, you might be tempted to think, "Well, I don't have any testimonies or any miracles." Girl, yes you do! You are alive, and you are loved. I don't know about you, but there are so many times that I SHOULD HAVE BEEN DEAD. Accepting Jesus as my Lord and Savior was a miracle for me, because my mom STAYED on her knees praying for me. The same applies to you. That is a miracle, and I promise that God has so many more in store for you.

Recalling what He has done for you will help you stay grateful and grounded. When you are ready to scream because you are so overwhelmed with stress from decisions, crazy people, tasks and deadlines, take a moment to reflect on who God is:

a Way Maker
a Miracle Worker
a Promise Keeper

God has had your back thus far, and He does not plan to go anywhere. If He has called you to something, then He will bring you through it. Knowing this will help you stay focused and at peace when the world is trying to drag you down.

I am actually experiencing this as I write this chapter. I had to give myself a pep talk today, which consisted of remembering who God is and changing my perspective on my season. I had to release my need to control my circumstances and lay it at the foot of the cross. No, it wasn't easy—it has actually taken me two weeks to get over my brat attack—but I have found that nothing will keep me grateful and grounded other than reflecting on who God is:

a Way Maker
a Miracle Worker
a Promise Keeper

He is all of that and more, so all that we need to do is just trust in Him. The moment we start feeling flustered, overwhelmed, or ready to quit, it means that we have taken things into our own hands. When we trust that God will work things out for our good, we can live in peace and sleep better. I know I start power tripping and control sipping when I am tired and when anxiety creeps up. I get exhausted because I keep thinking about the situation, trying to muster up solutions and ways to fix it. I try to think of every possible strategy to get me out of the problem. I call it forming strategies and solutions, but God calls it control. My sleep gets interrupted, I have dreams about the issue, and my mind goes around the problem over and over again.

Anxious thoughts and exhaustion do not come from God. There are a few times in the Bible that we are specifically told that Jesus took a nap, and you will find that God often encouraged people to take naps before embarking on long journeys or quests. Even the Sabbath was created for us to REST IN HIM, and we must rest if we want the fruit of Spirit (anxiety is not listed as one) to be evident in our lives.

Rest assured, that God has it all under control. You just need to allow Him to surprise you. If you do not like surprises, this might be a little difficult for you. If you have to know everything, please get ready for God to rock your lovely, perfectly planned world. Believe it or not, I don't like surprises. I am the type of person who will read the end of a novel to find out what happens. Spoilers aren't a problem for me. You could actually tell me what happened in a movie, and it would not bother me at all. Yet it is incredible when a surprise comes my way! When God blessed me at the last minute with a hefty donation of $1,000 to get me to Greece, I was thrilled! I had trusted that He would make a way, and He did. When God blessed me with a job that paid double what I had been getting at the job I had walked out on, I literally screamed with joy.

It is testimonies like mine and yours that prove the nature of God. He is consistent and faithful. If you have to play that song over and over, singing the words until you believe them, then do it. Do whatever it takes for you to know that He is a way maker, miracle worker, and a promise keeper.

Chapter Thirteen Reflections

1. Did you like the song? How did you feel when you were listening to it? Did God show you anything while you worshipped Him? Write it down.

_____

_____

_____

_____

_____

2. What has God done in your life thus far? How does this prove that He is indeed a way maker, miracle worker and a promise keeper?

_____

_____

_____

_____

_____

3. What are you currently believing God for? What does He need you to do or to release?

Chapter 14
REMAINING HIS

They drifted slowly, sometimes connecting with each other and sometimes remaining content to float in isolation. I lay back on the couch in my apartment's courtyard to take in the beauty of the clouds. Why was I so fascinated by them? I could spend all day watching them. It was a pretty day, and I had nothing planned. The only thing keeping me from remaining outside all day was the Texas heat. At some point, I knew that I would start to complain about my neck getting sticky or a mosquito biting me, yet I remained in that moment, breathing in the fresh air while listening to the birds chirping around me.

My mind drifted to heaven, and I began to imagine how magnificent clouds must look there. Would we be able to chill in them and float across the sky or would there be something more fascinating than clouds for me to enjoy? God had already proven Himself to be an incredible artist with the work He had done here on Earth, so I couldn't even begin to wrap my mind around what heaven would be like. It didn't take long before I began to wonder why I was still stuck on Earth. I wanted to experience paradise with Jesus. I didn't want to go back to reality, dealing with crazy people, or facing the temptations of my flesh. I felt ready for heaven. But God wasn't ready for me to come to heaven yet, and the same is probably true for you, too.

Oftentimes we wonder how we can possibly live like Jesus while on Earth. I know this is something I find myself asking God to help me with, because if I am being honest, it is not always easy. It doesn't matter if you have attended church every Sunday for your entire life or if you are new in your walk with God. Every day, we all deal with the challenges of loving other people, staying faithful to God, and truly living like Jesus. So, how do we remain His while we're here dealing with drama, heartache, and a chaotic culture? How do I continue being faithful to God and His purposes for my life when my season looks completely dry and defeated?

When we accept Jesus as our Savior and decide to make Him Lord of our lives, we become His. We become His even if we don't truly understand what it means to be His child. We remain His by staying close to Him and inviting Him into our everyday lives. It isn't about perfect church attendance, following some rule book, or condemning others who live their lives differently. No, that is not how you remain His. You remain His by inviting Jesus and the Holy Spirit to be a part of your life. Every. Single. Day.

Whether you need to make a big decision that requires a ton of wisdom from God or you're dealing with something on a simpler scale, God wants you to invite Him into your life. We remain fruitful, healthy, whole, and true to our identity, when we remain in Him. The moment we choose to ditch Jesus and go with our feelings or what our flesh wants, we depart from Him. For example, when God told me that I couldn't be my ex-girlfriend's friend, He made it clear to me what I would be deciding if I chose to disobey Him. Ultimately, I would be living as a branch that has been broken from the tree, withered away on the ground. A branch separated from its tree becomes lifeless because it is no longer connected to its source of life, as the tree provided the branch nutrients and a place to grow. Likewise, when we walk away from God, we are walking away from our source of nourishment.

Had I disobeyed God, after receiving this revelation, I would have chosen my flesh, instead of His everlasting love. Again, this was difficult for me to understand, because I couldn't understand why He would God make me choose if He really loves me. Simply said, God needs to have all of my heart, mind, and my soul. The idea of a commitment and a covenant was brand new to me, but I knew that if I wanted to experience God in deeper levels of my life, I needed to remain in His will for my life.

With that said, remaining in His will is going to be challenging, if you have dealt with rebellion at some point in your life. I'm not sure if you have noticed by reading this book, but I am talking about myself here. I was rebellious towards my parents, school teachers, the law, and even to God. So, when God lovingly corrects me or commands my obedience, it can be challenging for me at times. These moments are typically when brat attacks arise. But I know that the more I practice obedience and draw near to Him, the easier it will be for me to joyfully obey Him and remain in His will.

Remaining His is also about showing up every day. It is hard to get to know anyone without spending time with them. When you are introduced to a potential boo or a new friend, I have no doubt that you are intentional about spending time with them. Why wouldn't you be? You want to get to know them, therefore you make it a priority to hang out with them. And once you identify who they are, you make the decision to either keep them in your life or dismiss them from your life. Typically, if you end up enjoying the time that you spend together, you keep showing up and making plans to connect.

The same thing applies to God. If we desire to get to know Him, we have to spend time with Him. It is only in those times, when it's just the two of you, that you will begin to fall in love with His character, His nature, and even His artistic abilities. This depth of love is what will keep you going when things get tough. There are so many people who like the concept of Jesus and His love, but they end up breaking up with Him as soon as they face a few challenges, experience His correction, or if they have bad experiences with immature Christians. Jesus uses a parable in Matthew 13:1-44 to further explain what these two lifestyles look like, that I would encourage you to read.

If you are reading this and you have broken up with God before, come back to Him. Like in the story of the father and the prodigal son, God has His arms wide open, ready to embrace you. And His embrace is comforting even amongst the many trials that you are facing or have yet to face.

Remaining His is difficult if you are always on the verge of cussing people out. Trust me, I know. Remaining His requires us to learn how to see people through the lens of compassion. It requires us to seek to understand, not to be understood. It requires us to be slow to speak, really taking our time to think before we speak. It also requires us to protect our brothers' and sisters' names, refusing to entertain gossip. It sometimes requires for you to pray for those who persecute you. This will not happen naturally immediately, especially if you are a former gangsta like myself. But again, the more you spend time with Jesus, the more you will resemble Him.

Remaining in Christ does not mean that you should hold yourself to a high standard, only to point out the plank in other people's eyes, nor does it give you the right to be blatantly disrespectful to people who live their lives differently than you. Unfortunately, a huge chunk of society has been hurt by immature church folk, and as a result, they have completely dismissed Jesus. Hang in there with me, though. I am not saying that you cannot evangelize or speak your beliefs; I am simply encouraging you to show people who God is through your actions and the way that you love people. If I was introduced to Jesus by hearing "You're a stripper going to hell" or anything that sounded even remotely judgmental, I would not be here right now, and the book in your hands would be replaced by the half-naked pictures that I used to post on my Instagram account.

Remaining in Christ means learning how to connect with everyone. Jesus did not shy away from the truth, but He made an effort to connect with people individually, making His message resonate with them in a way that they would comprehend. He did not run up to people pointing fingers or passing out tickets to hell. My deepest hope and prayer is that we learn how to love and live with people who do not believe in Jesus. I personally am believing that God will show me how to reach specific people based off of their needs and personalities. And as I remain in Him, He will reveal this knowledge to me and equip me with love and understanding.

And lastly, I believe remaining in Christ means loving yourself through the lens of how your Father sees you. He sees you as His masterpiece (Ephesians 2:10). This means speaking kindly to and about yourself; loving every freckle, pimple, dimple, and detail about yourself. This WILL be a journey for you. It has been for myself. I have learned how to love every imperfection about myself because of God. A once perfectionist, obsessed with fitting in and getting attention, is now living her best life with Jesus and those who love her authentically and genuinely. Because I am loved, and so are you.

We have so many things in this world that demand our attention and influence the way that we think about ourselves. More and more women are getting plastic surgery to try to meet the standard of beauty that they see on social media. More and more women are choosing to go after careers that literally have nothing to do with their purpose. More and more women are allowing themselves to be belittled by other women, due to their own insecurities. More and more women love themselves on social media but hate who they are in their real life.

If we not only become His, but we remain His, we learn to love ourselves. We see ourselves in a unique light. We stop comparing ourselves, we stop competing, and we stop hating on others and ourselves. When we are living loved and unbothered, we are living our best lives. We are truly remaining in Him.

BEGIN THIS JOURNEY by asking God how He sees you. Get a journal, light some candles, and create some romantic ambiance in the room. Allow God to romance you in this moment. I know it sounds spooky ooky, and it could be a new concept to some of you, but Jesus calls us His bride, so let's talk to Him like a hubby. Ask Him how He *sees* you, and invite Him to lead you into a new season of life. Welcome this season with open arms, because I promise you, when you get even a little hint of how God truly sees you, you will live and love better.

What do you love?

What do you dislike?

What brings you laughter, peace and joy?

Ask God to help you love yourself better by getting to know yourself through the lens in which He sees you. You will learn so much about yourself! And let's be real, we love to spend lots of time with ourselves. Through Christ, you will fall in love with the woman that you are today as well as the woman that you are becoming. You will learn how to forgive yourself for mistakes that you made in the past, and you will no longer hate the person you were back then. Remaining in Christ gives you the ability to love God, yourself, and others wholly, truthfully and authentically. And what a beautiful way to live while we remain on Earth.

Epilogue

Since finishing the manuscript for this book, I have been so overwhelmed with emotions. While I am thrilled to publish the book and see how God uses it to transform lives, I have also been scared; scared of the publishing costs, scared of the negative feedback, and even scared of the backlash that might come from the enemy. But God hasn't given me a spirit of fear.

For God has not given us a spirit of fear,
but of power and of love and of a sound mind.

- 2 Timothy 1:7 (NKJV)

Our heavenly Father hasn't given either one of us a spirit of fear. Fear comes from the enemy. So, if you are reading this right now, it is because I chose to stand on truth and boldly move forward with the task that God gave me. I decided to claim what God had already shown me to be mine. I encourage you to do the same.

Fear will always try to come back and choke you out. Vivid description, right? Well, that is because fear doesn't approach you light-heartedly. Instead of shrinking back and hiding, do the opposite of what fear is telling you to do.

If God told you to start a business, but fear is making you worry about income and resources, then start the business.

If God is leading you to end a toxic relationship, but fear makes you feel lost without him or her, then end the relationship.

If fear is telling you to isolate yourself because you can't trust anyone, seek God on how to freely love and trust again.

Do the opposite of what fear is telling you to do. That is how you win.

Now that I have completed this manuscript, God has shown me what I need to be praying and believing for next. Once again, it is something bigger than myself, and it will require a lot of faith. It is beyond what I have done before, but I know that God will provide, as I trust Him with the next step. It will also require a ton of love, grace and patience with the people in my life. As you probably know by now, these haven't always been my strongest suits. I share this with you to show you that like yourself, I am still on this journey… every single day. Some days are better than others, and I applaud myself for being more like Jesus. But then there are days where my tolerance is low or my faith is tested. On these days, I just have to remember that Jesus still loves me. He still cheers me on, draws me in with His grace and love, and whispers truth to me. And if you are on the same journey as myself, just know that He still loves you too.

Acknowledgements

To my mom, Gloria Mansfield – You have prayed, fought and believed with your entire existence for my salvation. You have had front row seats to most of the things (both good and bad) that I have experienced in my life. You prayed fervently, even while I was on a motorcycle to hell, and now you not only see the answers to your prayers, but you have also witnessed God completely transform me. Thank you for loving me, challenging me, and for believing in me.

To Amanda & Cory Roberts – Thank you for being the catalyst to my salvation. You both showed me how to truly love God and others who live differently. When you met me, I was a lost, angry, and confused young woman. I was searching for answers and for love. You both introduced me to an everlasting love, and I am so grateful that God put you two in my life. Thank you for being the stepping stone into my relationship with Jesus Christ.

To SESTER, Naja Wade – I would not want any other woman to be my sister. Thank you for always encouraging me to keep pursuing my dreams, even the wild and large dreams that most people would frown upon. This book is one of the many dreams, and you saw my struggle to write it. You cheer me on even when I lose sight of the vision (barely happens, but you get my point). Your encouragement and support isn't unnoticed. Love you, sester!!

To Leah Albright Bryd – You are just an overall blessing in my life, girl! This book aside, you inspire me and add refreshment to my life. God knows I have always wanted a big sister, but to have a big sister who has a similar story to mine?! That's GOLD! Thank you for being an incredible big sis to me. During this book writing process, you have seen me cry, hurt, and heal. And as long as I invited you into my heart, you were right there each time. Even when I didn't want to be vulnerable, you still give me the space I needed, yet remained close enough for me to call. You celebrated and got excited with me once I finished this book, and God knows how important that is to me. Thank you, big sis.

To Brie Brown- Brie, girl! I love you dearly :) Thank you for being the voice of truth when I was stuck, trying to decide if I was going to trust God and leave the strip club. You have been a part of my journey the longest. From being a hood hot mess in high school, to being Holy/hood current day, I am grateful that I have had a close friend grow alongside me in this journey. I appreciate your hunger to grow, dream, and to love wholly. Thank you for embracing me.

To Alex Marshall-Grant – Like literalllllyyy (you know how I am saying this), you are a godsend! First of all, we met in London, which automatically makes our friendship cool, but on top of that, you UNDERSTAND ME. I have never had someone understand me as well as you do! And wow, God knows that you are a gift to me! Thank you so much for being available, even though you live across the WORLD. As you read along, you probably had a whole lot of "Girl, I remember this" moments! And you should, because I ran to you often because I felt (and still feel) safe talking to you. I love you, girl. Oh, and God said to move to the U.S. (kidding).

To Brittney Freeman – You are such an expression of God's goodness and joyfulness. I am so blessed by your friendship, goofiness, encouragement, and support. You are consistently compassionate, and you never fail to provide what I need in a friend. Thank you for always being my cheerleader, warrior friend! Thank you for praying with me during this process, comforting me as I heal throughout my journey, and for the fun times that we always have together. I love you and value all of who you are, girl!

To Terasha Burrell, I am so thankful that we had a connection in Greece that continued to grow once we returned to our homes. You have been my writing accountability partner, an inspiration to heal deeper, and a supportive friend throughout the short amount of time that I have known you. I love you and can't wait to see where God takes our friendship.

To Kyaris Brown- Oh my sweet friend, Kyaris. Why are we so different yet so alike?! I appreciate everything about you and love your heart for God. You not only desire Jesus, but you truly want people to experience His love on an intimate level. You have inspired my walk with God, helped me grow into my purpose and have been such a fun joy to do life with! I love you, sis.

To Rhiannon Payne- My truth seeker and loving friend. Thank you for being a part of my transformation and healing journey. You've spent so many phone calls and conversations being a listening ear and support. Thank you for encouraging me to always seek God's truth. I love you and value your heart, purpose, dreams and desires.

To Stephani McDaniel – Back in 2016 at the FIRE Conference you were the first person to encourage me to write this book. You sat with me as I shared my testimony. I was NOT trying to write about my story at the time, yet God used you as a prophetic voice to speak it into existence, and three years later, the book you are holding has been birthed. Thank you, Stephani.

To Victoria Guerra, TaShuana Davis, Anna Holman, Faith McGhee, Carrie Thomas, Brittan Jobe, Jeremy Boykin, Juliette Bush, Karolyne Roberts, Brittany Parker, Reginald Turner, S'ambrosia Wasike, and Janaye Jordan – Thank you for being a part of this journey with me. Each of you impact me in such a tremendous way, and your support doesn't go unnoticed. Thank you for checking on me, challenging me, and for allowing me to be my authentic self. From my friends, to my book publishing team, you are all so loved and valued! Thank you again.

Resources
FOR SHARING YOUR STORY

To those who have a story to tell, this is for you. So, basically, I'm talking to anyone who is holding this book, because unless you grew up with a perfect, storm-free life, we all have a story to tell.

I have so much joy as I am writing these last few pages, because this process has been unpredictable and challenging, yet wildly refreshing for me. And I actually have completed that which I set my heart to do! I WROTE THIS BOOK!! If you know me personally, then you know how much this means to me.

Anyway, while I hope that this book has blessed you, I know that it has brought healing in my own life. Writing my story has exposed places in my heart that needed forgiveness and the love of God. This whole process has brought me closer to God for the simple fact that writing a book is not easy—especially a book that makes the enemy mad! I have had to lean on God, relying on His strength to lift me up when I wanted to quit.

When I cried myself to sleep or woke up due to being taunted by the enemy, Jesus held my hand every step of the way. When facing trauma or recalling images I had once suppressed, God embraced me as His daughter.

If you have a book, a movie, or a video to share that highlights the glory of God in your life, I want you to go after it. Do not allow fear or the enemy's punk self to keep you stuck in his lies. God will never leave you hanging. He will be with you the ENTIRE way. Even if you find yourself procrastinating (which I did often), He will be with you.

   I believe that God will show you what to share and what to keep between the two of you. Believe it or not, I did not give you every detail of my life story, because I was not led to do so. And praise God! I love that some things were left to me in private. But I do know that God wants to share your story for His glory. But how do we do that? This is an outline of what I was given by a former mentor, and going through this process has helped me share my story many times.

- **Where you were** – stripping, rebellious teen, fighting, jail
- **What you saw/felt** – detached, lonely, anger, misunderstood
- **What God did/what happened** – healed my dad, met Cory & Amanda, started to desire Jesus
- **What God has done/is going to do** – new identity, healing, breakthroughs in all areas, dream trip, finished my first book, healthy relationships

This outline may or may not work for you. Regardless, you know in your heart if God is telling you to write about your story and share your experiences with others. Whatever it takes for you to get your story on paper, just do it! It will bring a deeper layer of healing to your own heart as you walk alongside others in the journey of becoming the women God has created them to be.

Quick Prayers
FOR WRITING/SHARING YOUR STORY

"Lord, help me to write my book without the need to be perfect. Help me extend grace towards myself and keep my mind focused on saving souls."

"God, give me a sharp mind, a compassionate heart, and a quick ear to hear the Holy Spirit as I write and share my story."

"I rebuke any attacks, cancel assignments from the enemy and rebuke every curse spoken against me in Jesus' name."

"God, grant me your strength, supernatural peace, joy and focus as I write."

"Thank you for favor and provision, and for giving me a team of supporters during this journey."

Scriptures
FOR THE SOUL

Isaiah 26:3 (NLT) "You will keep in perfect peace all who trust in you, all whose thoughts are fixed on you."

Psalms 119:45 "I will walk in freedom, for I have devoted myself to your commandments."

Psalms 119:36-37 "Give me an eagerness for your laws rather than a love for money! Turn my eyes from worthless things and give me life through your word."

John 15 THE ENTIRE CHAPTER

Luke 22:42-43 "'Father, if you are willing, please take this cup of suffering away from me. Yet I want your will to be done and not mine.' Then an angel from heaven appeared and strengthened him."

Matthew 5:8 "Blessed are those whose hearts are pure, for they will see God."

Proverbs 3:5-6 "Trust in the Lord with all of your heart; do not depend on your own understanding. Seek His will in all that you do, and He will show you which path to take."

James 4:7 "So humble yourself before God, resist the devil and he will flee."

Psalms 40 THE ENTIRE CHAPTER

Ephesians 3:20 "Now to Him who is able to do immeasurably more than all we ask or imagine, according to His power that is at work within us."

Ephesians 2:10 "For we are God's masterpiece. He has created us anew in Christ Jesus so that we can do the good things He has planned for us long ago."

Ephesians 2:13 "But now you have been united with Christ Jesus. Once you were far away from God, but now you have been brought near to Him through the blood of Jesus Christ."

Philippians 2:13 "For God is working in you, giving you the desires and the power to do what pleases Him."

Philippians 4:6-7 "Don't worry about anything, but instead pray about everything. Tell God what you need, and thank Him for what He has already done. Then you will experience God's perfect peace, which exceeds anything that we can understand. His peace will guard your hearts and mind as you live in Christ Jesus."

James 1:2-3 "Dear brothers & sisters, when troubles of any kind come your way, consider it an opportunity for great joy. For you know that when your faith is tested, your endurance has a chance to grow. So let it grow, for when endurance is fully developed, you will be perfect and complete, lacking nothing."

James 1:14 "Temptation comes from our own desires, which entice us and drag us away. These desires give birth to sinful actions. And when sin is allowed to grow, it gives birth to death."

James 1:26 "If you claim to be religious, but don't control your tongue, then you are fooling yourself and your religion is worthless."

1 Peter 5:8 "Stay alert! Watch out for your great enemy, the devil. He prowls around like a roaring lion looking for someone to devour. Stand firm against him, and be strong in your faith."

Romans 8:1 "There is no condemnation for those who belong to Christ Jesus."

Romans 8:31 "If God is for us, then who can ever be against us?"

Romans 8:38 "And I am convinced that nothing can separate us from God's love. Neither death nor life, neither angels nor demons, neither our fears for today nor our worries about tomorrow-not even the powers of hell can separate us from God's love."

Matthew 16:24-25 "Then Jesus said to his disciples, "Whoever wants to be my disciple must deny themselves and take up their cross and follow me. For whoever wants to save their life will lose it, but whoever loses their life for me will find it."
2 Corinthians 5:17 "Therefore, if anyone is in Christ, the new creation has come: The old has gone, the new is here."

Isaiah 54:17 "No weapon forged against you will prevail, and you will refute every tongue that accuses you. This is the heritage of the servants of the Lord, and this is their vindication from me," declares the Lord."

Proverbs 13:20 "Walk with the wise and become wise, for a companion of fools suffers harm."

Galatians 5:1 "It is for freedom that Christ has set us free. Stand firm, then, and do not let yourselves be burdened again by a yoke of slavery."

John 8:36 "So if the Son sets you free, you will be free indeed."

Galatians 6:9 "Let us not become weary in doing good, for at the proper time we will reap a harvest if we do not give up."

Jeremiah 33:3 "Call to me and I will answer you and tell you great and unsearchable things you do not know."

About Imani

Imani Wade is a fur-baby momma, loving both her dog and cat. If not writing, or working towards her dreams, she is chasing palm trees and planning her next vacation. Her feisty personality, that once got her into a lot of fist fights and jail time, is now being used to fight for others and the Kingdom of God. Her hustler mindset, that once influenced her to turn to the strip clubs, is now used to help dreamers brainstorm income streams. Her trust issues that she had with men, that led her to hating them and turning to women, is now being used to pray for men and share God's light on others who can relate to same-sex attraction. And the little girl who once loved to write, creating storylines beyond her age or experience, is now being used to write and to share her own story.

-Connect with Imani-

Instagram: imaniinspires
YouTube: Imani Wade

Made in United States
North Haven, CT
08 June 2022